MORE THAN

PETTICOATS

REMARKABLE
WASHINGTON
WOMEN

L.E. Bragg

TWODOT

A · TWODOT · BOOK

© 1998 by Falcon® Publishing, Inc., Helena, Montana
Printed in Canada.

  3 4 5 6 7 8 9 10 TP 05 04 03 02 01 00

Cover photo: Women's Relief Corps, 1885. Courtesy Museum of History and Industry.

Design, typesetting, and other prepress work by Falcon® Publishing, Inc., Helena, Montana.
Visit our website at http://www.falconguide.com.

Library of Congress Cataloging-in-Publication Data

Bragg, L. E. (Lynn E.), 1956-
     More than petticoats : remarkable Washington women / L.E. Bragg.
        p.   cm.
     "A Twodot book."
     Includes bibliographical references and index.
     ISBN 1-56044-667-6
     1. Women—Washington (State)—History. 2. Women—Washington
(State)—Biography.   I. Title
     HQ1438.W2B74 1998
     305.4'092'2797—dc21   98-7356
                                                                                                        CIP

$\mathcal{I}$ accomplished what I have always dreamed of and feared impossible, and from my experience nothing could be taken.

Fay Fuller—after reaching the summit
of Mount Rainier on
August 10, 1890

$\mathcal{A}$CKNOWLEDGMENTS

$\mathcal{S}$pecial thanks to Joy Werlink of the Washington State Historical Society; Lisa Love of the *The News Tribune*; Nancy Gale Compau of the Spokane Public Library's Northwest Room; Karen De Seve of the Cheney Cowles Museum; and Carolyn J. Marr, librarian at the Museum of History and Industry. A large number of individuals also provided assistance for individual chapters; their names can be found in the bibliography under each chapter listing.

CONTENTS

PREFACE

Dedicated to my nineteenth century, Washingtonian great-grandmothers: Jessie Penola (Gordon) Bragg of Colfax, Washington; Hannah Mary "Marie" ("Von" Sapp) Eckles of Sunnyside, Washington; and Elizabeth (Paddock) Lee of Seattle, Washington. Not to be forgotten is Mary Ann (Johnston) Nixon of Ballymena, County Antrim, Northern Ireland. Thanks also to my Oregonian-Washingtonian mother, Mary Pauline "Polly" (Nixon) Bragg, for reading and editing every word I have ever written and to Elinor MacDonald for her help in editing this book.

The stories of the women found within these pages illustrate the unique history that made the state of Washington what it is today. Although the credit for building this great state usually is given to its male citizens, women played equally important roles. These sixteen women, all of whom were either born in or migrated to Washington in the nineteenth to early twentieth centuries, epitomize the spirit of the Northwest.

It was my goal to tell the stories of an ethnically and geographically diverse group of women from a great variety of vocations, including a doctor, a lawyer, and the daughter of an Indian chief. Their lives of courage, dedication, and achievement laid the foundation for the Washington of today. Professor Edmond S. Meany's famous statement about Seattle could well be said for all of Washington, "The foundation of Seattle was laid in a mother's tears." Some died tragically, some fell from grace, some are still revered and remembered, while others forgotten. This book is intended to honor the memories of these remarkable Northwest women. ❧

Narcissa Prentiss Whitman

Narcissa Prentiss Whitman

1808–1847

Massacre at Waiilatpui

The deadly blade of the tomahawk, previously cloaked beneath the Cayuse's blanket, dealt two sharp blows to the back of the doctor's head, knocking him senseless to the floor of the tiny mission kitchen. Seventeen-year-old John Sager drew his pistol upon the intruders. One of the Indians, now swarming into the kitchen, grabbed the gun barrel before John could shoot and stabbed him in the head. Telaukaikt (who had been studying to become a member of the church) later entered the room and began to beat and cut the doctor about the head and face, leaving him with his throat cut— life pouring out of him. Mortally wounded, both Dr. Marcus Whitman and John Sager lived only until nightfall.

Gun shots began to ricochet about the mission yard. Upon hearing the shots, Narcissa Whitman ran to the kitchen and came upon her fallen husband. Narcissa bent over her bloodied mate, attempting to comfort him. Tears of fear and grief flowed together with her spouse's blood. She and another woman moved Dr. Whitman from the kitchen floor to a couch in the parlor.

Mr. Rogers, a young missionary, escaped from his attackers in the yard with a broken arm and bloody head wound. He rushed into the house, shutting the door in a feeble attempt to keep out the hostile invaders. Mr. Kimball, his arm broken as well, joined Mr. Rogers in barricading themselves in an upstairs bedroom.

Still anguishing over her dying husband, Mrs. Whitman attempted to quiet the terrified screams of the mission's children. Crying children flew around the house in panic. As Narcissa passed by a window in order to reach the children, she was shot through the right breast by a Canadian of mixed blood named Joe Lewis. Her body crumpled to the floor. She sat up and dragged herself to the settee where her husband lay. Here, Sister Whitman commenced to pray for the lives of all at the Whitman Mission, especially the children.

*　*　*

Narcissa Prentiss was born in Prattsburg, New York, on March 14, 1808, the eldest daughter and third of nine children born to Judge Stephen Prentiss and Clarissa Prentiss. She grew up and attended school in Prattsburg and was a member of the first class of girls to attend Franklin Academy, a seminary school for women in Troy, New York. Following her graduation, Narcissa taught school.

In 1832, four Flathead Indian leaders visited St. Louis to encourage teachers to come live among them and teach them of "The Book of Truths." Their speeches were published in the *Christian Advocate* in March of 1833 and stirred great excitement in the East. At age twenty-six, Narcissa attended a meeting where the Reverend Samuel Parker, a missionary explorer for the American Board of Commissions for Foreign Missions, made an appeal for missionaries and money to support his goal of establishing missions among western Indian tribes. Narcissa felt her true calling. She approached the Reverend Parker and asked if there was a place for an unmarried female among his western missionaries. Both the Reverend Parker and Narcissa Prentiss made a request of the board to allow her to travel west as a missionary. The board denied the requests, thinking the West an unsuitable match for a single woman.

A young medical doctor, Marcus Whitman, was slated to travel with Parker on his expedition. When the two met to plan the journey, Parker mentioned Narcissa Prentiss and her great desire to perform missionary work among western tribes. Further, Parker suggested that if Whitman was serious about becoming a missionary and wanted a wife, he should contact this woman and propose marriage. A month later Narcissa and Marcus were engaged to be married. Narcissa reapplied to the missionary board, not as a single female, but as a missionary wife.

Meanwhile, Dr. Marcus Whitman and the Reverend Samuel Parker set out on their expedition to explore the possibility of building missions in the Oregon Territory (which at that time encompassed the present-day states of Oregon, Washington, and Idaho). This territory was not part of the United States, but was held jointly with England and virtually ruled by the English Hudson's Bay Company.

Marcus and Samuel traveled as far west as Rendezvous, on the Green River in Wyoming. Here, the two decided that Samuel would go west to select sites for missions, while Marcus would return to New York for additional recruits. Marcus left Rendezvous on August 27, 1835, with two Nez Perce Indian boys, Richard and John, as guides. He had six months to recruit a party to join the American Fur Company's caravan, a safe party with whom to travel to Rendezvous in 1836.

When Marcus returned to New York, he and Narcissa were married on February 18, 1836. Richard and John attended the wedding, where they sat mesmerized by the ceremony. Narcissa, who sang soprano in her church choir, filled the church with her golden soprano voice as she sang the last stanza of her final wedding song.

The next day they left on their honeymoon—a three-thousand-mile trip to the Oregon Territory. With them were Reverend Henry H. Spalding; his wife, Eliza; William H. Gray; two teamsters; and, the two Nez Perce boys. Narcissa grew to love John and Richard, who proved to be excellent guides and took good care of the stock. The two hired men proved much less useful.

At first, the Whitman party traveled in the relative comfort of boats. From Pennsylvania, they cruised on the Ohio, Mississippi, and Missouri Rivers. The plan was to meet the American Fur Company caravan at Council Bluff and travel in the company of several hundred men and six hundred animals to the Oregon Territory. The men of the American Fur Company heard that women were in the party that was to join them. Not wanting to travel with females, the group moved out earlier than planned, leaving without the Whitman party.

Discouraged, but undaunted, Dr. Whitman and his group decided to go alone and try to catch the American Fur Company expedition. After a month of traveling, the small party caught up with the caravan.

Although they encountered many dangers and treacherous terrain while crossing the plains, the journey agreed with Narcissa Whitman. In a letter to her family, she wrote, "Our manner of living is far preferable to any in the States. I never was so contented and happy before. Neither have I enjoyed such health for years."

When in buffalo country, members of the American Fur Company caravan were designated hunters and were assigned to supply the meat—a diet of buffalo, antelope, deer, bear, and birds. Buffalo jerky and tea were sometimes the main meal. Eliza Spalding became sick on the diet; in contrast, Narcissa developed quite a taste for buffalo meat.

They began their ascent of the Rocky Mountains at South Pass, a natural road discovered by early trappers. Crossing the pass meant driving over dangerous, narrow, steep passages. For this reason, the party decided to leave the larger wagon behind. The women, who had alternated between riding in the wagon and on horseback, would now spend more time astride a mount. Narcissa preferred to ride horseback and so spent the rest of the journey in the saddle. In this manner, Narcissa and Eliza became the first white women to cross the Continental Divide.

The first tribe the missionaries saw was the Pawnee. Like other tribes they later encountered, the Pawnee were fascinated with the white women—the first they had ever seen. Narcissa wrote that when they arrived at Rendezvous, Wyoming, she was greeted warmly with kisses from the Indian women. A mountain man, Isaac P. Rose, described such a scene in his autobiography, *Four Years in the Rockies*:

> Mrs. Whitman was a large, stately, fair skinned woman, with blue eyes and light, auburn, almost golden hair. Her manners were at once dignified and gracious. She was by both nature and education, a lady, and had a lady's appreciation of all that was courageous and refined, yet not without an element of romance and heroism in her disposition strong enough to have impelled her to undertake a missionary's life in the wilderness. Mrs. Spalding, the other lady, was more delicate than her companion, yet equally earnest and zealous in the cause they had undertaken. The Indians would turn their gaze from the dark haired, dark eyed Mrs. Spalding to what was to them the more interesting golden hair and blue eyes of Mrs. Whitman. . . .

The American Fur Company traveled only as far as Rendezvous. A group of Nez Perce Indians offered to guide the party to Fort Walla Walla along a steep mountainous northern route. Wagons and stock would have to be left behind, and the Whitmans feared they would not be at Fort Walla Walla before winter. Soon, a party from the Hudson's Bay Company's Fort Vancouver base arrived at Rendezvous and offered the Whitman party a shorter route through desert terrain. Members of the Flathead, Nez Perce, and Snake tribes guided the Whitman party, now including members of the Hudson's Bay Company, to Fort Hall (Idaho). There, the Indians went north to their preferred route, while the missionaries and members of the Hudson's Bay Company traveled west.

After leaving Rendezvous, the travelers were far less likely to encounter parties traveling east, by whom they sent letters home to their families; so, Narcissa began to keep a journal chronicling her life on the trail. In it, she wrote that she found travel with the Indians more difficult than it had been with the fur company. The fur traders made two stops per day, while the Indians were accustomed to making camp only once a day.

Again, the party traveled on mountain trails, some described as so narrow a horse's hoof would barely fit on the trail. Some of the wagons slipped off the trail sending their contents tumbling down steep slopes. At some spots the wagons were eased over the mountainsides using long ropes. Much to everyone's dismay, Dr. Whitman insisted on bringing his wagon. When the trails became too narrow, his wife secretly hoped he would discard the contraption. Instead, the inventive doctor removed the front wheels, making the wagon into a cart. Later it was decided they should dispose of some of their belongings to lighten the wagon's load. Marcus convinced his bride that she must leave a treasured trunk, a gift from her sister.

After another month's journey through mountains, rivers, and deserts, the party arrived at Fort Walla Walla on September 1, 1836. When the pioneers arrived at their destination, Narcissa Whitman was nearly three months pregnant. In a letter to Samuel Parker dated

October 24, 1836, she wrote of her feelings about the journey:

> ... [Y]ou ask whether I regret coming by land? I answer
> No! by no means. If I were at home now, I could choose
> to come this way in preference to a seven month voyage.
> Nothing can equal the purity of the mountain air; and
> its exhilarating effect on the system; together with the
> healthful exercise of a horseback ride. Never have I slept
> more sweetly, than after a day thus spent. How unlike the
> close atmosphere of stages, boats, and disturbed rest of a
> crowded cabin, together with such an appetite as one has
> in this traveling. I found so much pleasure, mixed with
> the little suffering and fatigue endured; that the fatigue is
> entirely forgotten. I once could not believe such a jour-
> ney could be made with so little inconvenience, to a lady,
> as I have experienced. I believe I was prepared for the
> worst, but happily have been disappointed. True! I have
> had some hindrances, and been hungry at times, because
> we had nothing but buffalo meat dried in the sun by the
> Indians to eat. ...

Once in the new territory, the first order of business was to
meet with the ruling authorities, the Hudson's Bay Company, head-
quartered at Fort Vancouver. This trip was made by boat, traveling
west on the waters of the Columbia River. Dr. McLoughlin, the
chief factor of the Hudson's Bay Company, was very impressed by
the rugged trip the doctor and his fair bride had made. He suggested that the Whitmans make their mission near Walla Walla, and
the Spaldings 125 miles to the east, at Lapwai (Idaho). Narcissa
and Eliza remained at Fort Vancouver while their husbands returned
east of the Cascade Mountains to start construction of the missions. While at Fort Vancouver, Narcissa instructed Dr. McLoughlin's

daughter in her school studies and music.

Mr. Spalding returned for the women a month and a half later, telling them homes had been finished enough to provide them shelter. The women arrived at the mission site to find little but a lean-to enclosing a fireplace and chimney. The structure had a floor of rough hewn boards, but not a door, window, or bit of furniture, not even a bed! The site for their home was a peninsula between the branches of the Walla Walla River and Touchet Creek. The local Cayuse Tribe called this place Wai-i-lat-pui (rye grass place). The mission was located twenty-five miles east of Fort Walla Walla. Each year additions were made to the main house and accompanying buildings. Marcus traveled up to 1,500 miles in search of timber. He built a small grist mill to provide corn, rye, and wheat meal. By 1839, the Whitmans had fenced 250 acres and cultivated 200 acres with grain. Forty to fifty Indian children ages seven through eighteen attended the mission school with Narcissa as their teacher. The Cayuse were attending Sunday church services quite regularly, with Narcissa leading the services when Marcus was away.

Marcus's efforts to instill Christian values in the Indians included trying to interest them in helping him build the mission. In Cayuse society it was traditional for the men to hunt, fish, and fight, while the women built and tended the homes. Although the local native men were intrigued with the mission church and school, they saw the construction of the buildings as women's work, and chose not to participate. Marcus attempted to induce the locals to build permanent homes, plow, plant, sow, and raise cattle or sheep even though this also was not their way. The Cayuse were a proud people, wealthy with horses, who traveled to different encampments each season following their food sources. At the camps they hunted, fished, and traded for salmon, deer, elk, and buffalo.

Although Narcissa showed great love for individual Indians, she regarded the majority of them as heathen, both because they had not been "saved" and because of conflicts between the two societies—Mrs. Whitman often found herself at odds with native custom. The mission was situated on Cayuse land and the Cayuse, therefore, recognized no boundaries, including doors. She became accustomed to them entering the kitchen unannounced but objected to their tendency to roam the house, bedrooms included. This clash of cultures caused some of the natives to regard Narcissa Whitman as haughty.

The custom of polygamy also disturbed the pious Mrs. Whitman. She believed that Indian wives were mistreated, and regretted that early in the mission years she had little contact with Cayuse women, as only the men ventured to Waiilatpui. One Cayuse man questioned Dr. Whitman's practice of taking his wife with him everywhere he went. Dr. Whitman tried to explain that his wife was his partner, but this explanation did not sit well. The Cayuse were displeased with the equal treatment Narcissa received.

On March 14, 1837 (the evening of Narcissa's own birthday), Alice Clarissa was born to Narcissa and Marcus Whitman. Alice Clarissa was born on Cayuse land, thus the Cayuse considered this first child born to American parents in the Oregon Territory their child. The baby had many visitors from chiefs and important tribal members on a daily basis. As Narcissa described in a letter to her parents on March 30, 1837,

> Fee-low-ki-ke, a kind, friendly Indian, called to see her the next day after she was born. [He] said she was a Cayuse ten-ni (Cayuse girl), because she was born on Cayuse wai-tis (Cayuse land). He told us her arrival was expected by all the people of the country—the Nez Perces, Cayuses and Walla Wallapoos Indians, and, now she has arrived, it would soon be heard of by them all; and we must write to our land and tell our parents and friends of it.

The whole tribe are highly pleased because we allow her to be called a Cayuse girl.

Alice Clarissa grew to be a very bright and talkative toddler. To the great delight of the Cayuse, Alice began to sing hymns and converse in the Indian languages surrounding her. Narcissa wrote in a letter home:

> Alice has become so familiar with [the Nez Perce hymns] that she is repeating some part of them most of the time. Situated as I am, I know not how I shall succeed in training her as I ought. So many Indians and children are constantly in and about our house, and recently I discover her much inclined to imitate and talk with them, or they with her. It makes them very much pleased to think she is going to speak their language so readily. They appear to love her much. The old chief Cut Lip says "he does not expect to live long, and he has given all his land to her."

Dr. and Mrs. Whitman made every effort to learn the local language, although he did better at it than she. To do this, they needed to spend time with the tribal members, who traveled a great deal. It was not unusual for the Whitman family to leave their home and camp with the tribes. Narcissa described one such occasion when her family traveled sixty-five miles and spent three cold, winter weeks camping with the Nez Perce. She wrote to her family of how much she enjoyed these encampments and felt the riding and camping outdoors agreed with Alice's health. They also thought that such close associations with the Indians afforded them more opportunity for converting them to Christianity, as well as learning their language and customs.

Unfortunately, Narcissa seemed to have been influenced by other missionaries to remove her child from such frequent contact with the Indians. They scolded her, telling her of "the evils of allowing her to learn the native language." Confused, Narcissa prayed about the matter and had decided to remove herself and her daughter from such daily contact when tragedy struck.

One evening in June of 1839, two-year-old Alice Clarissa disappeared while the evening meal was being prepared. A search ensued, and when two tin cups were found floating in the river, hope faded. The rescuers waded the river in a last hope of finding the baby alive before an old Indian man dove under water, found Alice, and brought her lifeless little body to the surface. Narcissa grieved incessantly, and her health began to fail, even though she believed the child to be in a better place.

When a boundary dispute between the United States and the British threatened the Oregon Territory, Marcus went to Washington, D.C. and met with President Tyler and Congress to convince them that the Oregon Territory was worth having. The Hudson's Bay Company had been successful in keeping the secrets of the Oregon Territory to themselves. It was in their best interest if the population of the East believed the land worthless. Unlike the missionaries, the company had no desire to change the way the Indians lived as long as they were kept in constant supply of rich fur pelts.

In Congress the view was expressed that, "The Oregon Territory was a barren worthless country fit only for wild beasts and wild men. . . . it is shut off by impassable mountains and a great desert which made a wagon road impossible." Whitman informed the legislators that it would be a mistake of enormous magnitude to listen to the enemies of American interests in Oregon. "Six years ago I was told there was no wagon road to Oregon, and it was impossible to take a wagon there, and yet in spite of pleading threats, I took a wagon over the road and have it now." Dr. Whitman's pleas were successful in reviving American interest in the vast territories comprising the present-day states of Oregon, Washington, and Idaho.

When Marcus returned in the spring, he had with him a large group of emigrants bound for Oregon—one thousand men, women, and children—and one thousand head of stock—cattle, horses, and sheep. The emigration that ensued, following Marcus Whitman's speech, brought the population of Americans up three-to-one over the British and Canadians in the territory.

Whitman foresaw the wealth and importance of the country and knew that his mission must serve as a supply station to the annual emigrations. As hundreds and thousands of emigrants came to the mission, worn, hungry, sick, and destitute, the Whitmans cared for them all. They provided them with food, clothing, and medicine, often without pay. Frequently, the doctor would give away his entire food supply and have to send to the Spaldings for grain to get them through the winter.

Meanwhile, Narcissa was called upon more and more to minister to wagon loads of emigrants now traveling to the Oregon Territory. Both Indian and white children were left as boarders at Waiilatpui, where Narcissa was the only teacher until she was assisted in later years by others. Narcissa also kept busy with a family of seven children who were placed in the Whitman's care after their parents had died on the trail west. The Whitmans legally adopted all seven of the Sager children though Dr. Whitman feared the emaciated baby would be too much of a burden on the frail Narcissa.

The Indians became increasingly dismayed by the huge influx of emigrants. They did not mind so much as long as the wagon trains were just passing through, but they did not want more settlers on their lands. Both the Hudson's Bay Company and the local tribes blamed Whitman for opening up the territory after his arrival with such a large caravan of emigrants. These feelings became even more pronounced when England lost the Oregon Territory through a treaty signed in 1846, ending the Hudson's Bay Company's domination of the territory.

In addition to the unrest among the natives, there was a growing animosity between the Protestant missionaries and the Catholic priests moving into the territory. Each group claimed theirs was the only true religion, thereby causing confusion and mistrust among the Indians.

Though they were spending more of their time on the needs of the settlers, the Whitmans were not unsympathetic to the plight of the Indians. Narcissa wrote, "We feel that we cannot do our work too fast to save the Indian—the hunted, despised and unprotected Indian—from entire extinction."

With the settlers came the white man's diseases. In 1847, a measles epidemic caused a great deal of sickness among both settlers and Indians. The Indians, who had little resistance to the disease, died in much greater numbers than the whites. The Cayuse were led to believe that Dr. Whitman was poisoning them.

One night, under the cover of darkness, Dr. Whitman's friend, Istikus, came to him. Risking his own life, Istikus told the doctor of threats against his life, advising him to leave the mission, "until my people have better hearts." Mrs. Whitman was devastated by the news. She locked herself in her room and cried all night. Though he refused to leave, Marcus realized the gravity of the situation and advised others at the mission to remove their families to safer places. It was the first time Marcus Whitman had been so alarmed or thought that his Indian friends could be capable of attempting such acts.

The next day, November 29, 1847, was like many others. Dr. Whitman had returned from ministering to Cayuse Indians who were sick with the measles, and he was now at rest, reading in the mission's small kitchen. Like most afternoons, the kitchen was filled to capacity with members of the Cayuse Tribe. It was under the guise of asking for medicine that the attackers entered the house, approached Dr. Whitman, and administered the blow that began the Whitman Massacre.

With Dr. Whitman's life ebbing away from the slash to his throat, the others convinced the wounded Narcissa to leave her husband's side and hide herself upstairs in a bedroom with Messrs. Rogers and Kimball and the women and children of the mission. They remained huddled in fear until well after dark. The sounds of breaking glass and shattering wood emanated throughout the house, as the attackers plundered through the Whitman's belongings. Several times the intruders climbed the stairs towards the terrified captives. Mr. Rogers found a broken gun barrel and thrust it through a crack in the door. The trick worked and he was able to fool them into thinking he was armed. With their original tactics not working, the Cayuse then attempted to coerce Mr. Rogers and Mrs. Whitman downstairs by alternately threatening to burn the house down and ensuring their safety if they did come down. The adults, fearing for the lives of the orphans, eventually agreed to descend the stairs. Narcissa, weak from loss of blood, fainted. Her limp figure was carried to a couch by Mr. Rogers and Miss Bewley. The rifles of the Cayuse who crowded into the room remained trained on the missionaries. As the settee containing the wounded Mrs. Whitman was carried outdoors, a volley of gunfire erupted both outside and within the house. Mr. Rogers and Mrs. Whitman were riddled with bullets. She groaned and fell to the ground, but still lingered on until mutilated by one of the raiders. Thus ended the life of a dedicated missionary wife and one of the first two, non-Indian women to cross the Continental Divide.

The leader of the massacre was the half-Indian Canadian Joe Lewis. It may have been his falsehoods which brought the conspiracy to the boiling point. Dr. Whitman had fed and clothed Lewis for months. Soon, the doctor discovered Joe's dishonesty and lack of character and tried to get rid of him. Joe Lewis returned and set about breeding distrust among the Cayuse. Several who took part in the killings had been frequent guests at the mission and had expressed interest in joining the church.

Thirteen people in all were killed, nine the first day—including Marcus and Narcissa (the only woman to die)—and four more over the next eight days. The last two men killed were dragged from their sick beds at the mission, beaten and stabbed before the eyes of the women and children who were now hostages at the mission. The mangled bodies were left by the door. For two days, the captives had to step over the dead to get food and water.

Forty women and children became hostages, later joined by two families to make the sum forty-seven. Several of the women were molested, and three were forced to become wives to their captors. Eliza Spalding, age ten, daughter of the Spaldings who had traveled west with the Whitmans, later described the constant horror and fear the hostages endured. She was forced to translate for her kidnappers, since she was fluent in their language.

When the chief factor of the Hudson's Bay Company, Peter Skene Ogden, heard of the massacre and the captives taken, he traveled to Fort Walla Walla, arriving on December 12. Ogden succeeded in ransoming all of the hostages with a supply of blankets, shirts, guns, ammunition, and tobacco. The total value of these goods was placed at approximately five hundred dollars.

No arrests were made until two years after the attack. Five Indian men were hung in Oregon City for participating in the Whitman Massacre, including one who evidently was not present there at all. Joe Lewis and another mixed-blood accomplice named Finley escaped to Montana, where it is said Lewis was killed some years later during a stagecoach robbery. The numbers of the Cayuse Tribe were greatly diminished by the epidemics, influx of settlers, and repercussions from their participation in the massacre. The Cayuse Tribe is now one of the Confederated Tribes of the Umatilla

Reservation, located near Pendleton, Oregon.

The Whitmans, who died for their cause of converting the Indians to Christianity, are remembered by some as martyrs. Samuel Campbell, who lived at the mission for two winters, never tired of telling

> of the grandly Christian character of Mrs. Whitman, of her kindness and patience to all, whites and Indians alike. Every evening she delighted all with her singing. Her voice, after all her hard life, had lost none of its sweetness, nor had her environments in any sense soured her toward any of the little pleasantries of every-day life. ❖

Mary Ann Boren Denny
1822–1910

Mother of Seattle

In preparation for the journey north from Portland to the Puget Sound country, the young mother, Mary Ann Denny, laundered her family's clothing and washed and starched her sun bonnet until the brim was properly stiff. She laid a cloth on the grassy ground and ironed her bonnet and dress so that she would appear well groomed for the trip.

Mary Ann, her husband Arthur, two young daughters—Louisa (seven) and Lenora (four)—and her newborn son, Rolland, who had been born in Portland just twelve days after her arduous four months of travel across the country by wagon train, set sail on the schooner *Exact* on November 5, 1851. Bound for Puget Sound with the Dennys were Mary's brother, Carson Boren, and his family; her sister, Louisa Boren; Arthur's brother, David Denny; the Low family, whom they had joined on the Oregon Trail; the Bell family, with whom they had become acquainted in Portland; and Charles and Lee Terry from New York by way of Olympia. With the twelve adults on the excursion were twelve children, all under the age of nine. The *Exact* was taking gold prospectors north to the Queen Charlotte Islands and settlers to Olympia, which was one of the few

Mary Ann Boren Denny

"settled" towns north of Portland.

As they waited to board the *Exact*, Mary bought salmon from local Indian vendors. There was a small cookstove aboard the ship, so the wives took turns cooking the fish for their family meals. Before they could even finish cooking, the women began to feel ill. One by one, men, women, and children became incapacitated by sea sickness. Whole families took to their bunks below deck as the ship was tossed and turned by the rolling sea.

The wind, which caused so much discomfort to the passengers of the tiny schooner, was a great boon in sailing up the Pacific coastline; just eight days after leaving Portland, the ship sailed into Puget Sound. The captain dropped anchor in the middle of the sound and sent his passengers ashore in rowboats. Mrs. Alexander, a passenger aboard the *Exact* headed for Olympia, described the women of the landing party in a newspaper interview:

> I can't never forget when the folks landed at Alki Point. I was sorry for Mrs. Denny with her baby and the rest of the women. You see, it was this way. Mr. Alexander and me went on to Olympia, but the rest stopped there. I remember it rained awful hard that last day—and the starch got took out of our bonnets and the wind blew, and every one of 'em, and their sun bonnets with the starch took out of them went flip flap, flip flap, as they rowed off for shore, and the last glimpse I had of them was the women standing under the trees with their wet bonnets all lopping down over their faces and their aprons to their eyes.

It was 8 A.M. on the morning of November 13, 1851, when the Denny party landed at Alki Point amid a typical Puget Sound winter storm. Winds howled and rain poured. The women and children of the party huddled on the rocky beach. Shivering with cold and drenched to the skin, their long calico frocks were plastered to their forms. The ship had already been partly shrouded by a curtain of driving rain, and they found themselves on a rocky shore at the base of a high sandy bank, with an endless expanse of dark, forbidding forests beyond that.

Mary Denny hugged her baby to her chest in a futile attempt to keep him warm and dry. The rain ran in rivulets from her limp bonnet. She and the other women sought shelter for their children as the men secured their household goods from the incoming tide.

Surely Arthur's brother, David, who had gone ahead to explore the Puget Sound region and had stayed there to build cabins for the families would have completed several homes for the group. Mary and the others were dismayed to find just one partially constructed log cabin, sans roof. They watched forlornly as the *Exact* sailed out of Puget Sound and out of sight. Baby in arms and daughters at her side, Mary Denny sat down on a soggy, fallen, old log and began to cry. Arthur Denny described the scene as he found his wife upon returning to Alki Beach:

> We were landed in the ship's boat when the tide was well out, and while the men of the party were all actively engaged in removing our goods to a point above high tide, the women and children had crawled into the brush, made a fire, and spread a cloth to shelter them from the rain. When the goods were secured I went to look after the women, and found on my approach, that their faces were concealed. On a closer inspection I found that they were in tears, having already discovered the gravity of the situation. . . . My motto in life was never to go backward and in fact if I had wished to retrace my steps it was about as nearly impossible as if I had taken up my bridge behind

me. I had brought my family from a good home, surrounded by comforts and luxuries and landed them in a wilderness, and I did not think it at all strange that a woman who had, without complaint, endured all the dangers and hardships of a trip across the great plains, should be found shedding tears when contemplating the hard prospects then so plainly in view.

Noted University of Washington history professor Edmond S. Meany aptly stated, "The foundation of Seattle was laid in a mother's tears," regarding Mary Denny's welcome to the area.

Members of Chief Seattle's* tribes—the Duwamish and Suquamish—witnessed the landing of the Denny party. They peered curiously from the woods, and some ventured cautiously onto the beach. An Indian mother showed Mary how to extract milk from the clams that were profuse on Alki Beach and how to nurse the baby with clam's milk. Mary Denny had been so sick during the trip from Portland, as well as stricken with fever in Portland, that she could not produce milk to feed her baby. Indian babies were often fed with the nectar of clams, on which they thrived, as it provided excellent nutrients. The baby, Rolland, was fed with clam nectar and broth until the party was able to bring its cattle north early the next year. The cattle had been left to winter in the Willamette Valley with Arthur Denny's father, who settled in Portland while the Dennys traveled north to the Puget Sound region.

The local Duwamish women were fascinated with the baby, Rolland. They stared intently at this tiny white skinned child, with light curly hair atop his head. Then they would shake their heads at the pale, fragile child and cluck their tongues, "Acha-da! Acha-da!

---

*Denny granddaughter, Roberta Frye Watt, reports that Chief Seattle himself was present when the Denny party first arrived at Alki. Other sources, including Arthur Denny's book, *Pioneer Days on Puget Sound*, do not mention Chief Seattle's presence on that day.

Memaloose—memaloose!" which is translated, "Too bad! Too bad! He die! He die!" In fact, Rolland lived well into old age as the last living member of the Denny party.

That night on Alki Point, twenty-four people and their belongings took cover from the pounding rain within the confines of the roofless cabin. Indian mats provided some shelter from the downpour. The Denny party's introductory night on Puget Sound left them wet, cold, and miserable by morning's light. This scene could not have been imagined by Mary Denny when she agreed to move west.

* * *

Mary Ann Boren was born November 25, 1822, in Nashville, Tennessee. In 1843, at the age of twenty, she married a young civil engineer, Arthur Armstrong Denny, and the couple settled in Illinois. Letters from friends who had ventured into the vast Oregon Territory enticed Arthur Denny to move his family west. Arthur had a good position as the county supervisor for Knox County, Illinois. Still, when the word came east of the Oregon Territory's virgin forests, majestic mountains, mild year-round climate, and fertile soil, Arthur Denny got the bug. However, Arthur would not uproot his wife and two young daughters unless Mary Ann would consent to the move. When he finally summoned up the courage to ask her, Mary agreed to go west.

As Mary and Arthur told family of their plans, the size of their traveling party increased. On April 10, 1851, Mary and Arthur, along with many in their extended families, left their home in Cherry Grove, Illinois. The Denny-Boren party included Arthur and Mary Denny with their two little daughters; Arthur's father, John Denny (a widower who had married Mary's mother, Sarah), wife, Sarah, and their baby daughter, Loretta; Arthur's four unmarried brothers,

James, Samuel, Wiley, and David; Mary's unmarried sister, Louisa Boren; and Mary's brother, Carson Boren with his wife and child. The group left Illinois in four wagons pulled by teams of horses and accompanied by a few head of cattle and two dogs. These brave pioneers left behind comfortable homes to venture west into the new Northwest territory.

In an attempt to retain some of the refinement of her home in Illinois while on the trail, Mary set the table properly for supper each evening, made up the beds with linen sheets for her family, and changed into nightclothes before retiring. One ferocious storm changed all of this by drenching their linens, bedding, and clothing thoroughly. From then on, the pioneers were so fatigued at the end of a day's travel that they gratefully fell into their bedrolls wearing whatever they had on at the time.

Conventions were often lost on the Oregon Trail. Mary's shoes soon wore out, and she finished the journey wearing buckskin moccasins. One of her daughters lost her only pair of shoes, so the two little girls were forced to share a single pair. They took turns wearing the shoes—one going barefoot, as the other went shod.

The small wagon train endured many hardships and dangers while crossing the barren plains, climbing winding mountain trails, and traveling through hostile Indian territory. The women bravely bore their travails. Mary Ann Denny was pregnant with her third child throughout the journey and not long after leaving Illinois, her two daughters came down with whooping cough. In addition to her trailside duties, Mary now had two children to nurse. The young mother worried about the lack of clean water and fresh fruits and vegetables to feed her little girls. Biscuits cooked over campfires and wild game were their staples.

The Denny party encountered additional hazards along the Oregon Trail: scorching deserts, sudden storms, droughts, rattlesnakes, wild animals, quicksand, stampeding of their own livestock, and an attack by a warring tribe. After four months of such grueling overland travel and a treacherous ride down the Columbia River, the party arrived in Portland on August 22, 1851. Once in Portland, members of the party, including Arthur and Mary, became gravely ill with malaria.

While on the trail, Arthur heard tales of the Puget Sound region from another traveler. When they arrived at their original destination in the Willamette Valley around Portland, they found it to be already inhabited by settlers. The members of the Denny-Boren party decided that John Low and David Denny would go north and explore the region. Along the route they were joined by Lee Terry in Olympia and while there, met Captain Robert Fay, who took them by boat to Puget Sound.

When Low, Denny, and Terry arrived on the shores of Elliott Bay on September 25, 1851, they found an encampment of Indians on the beach, fishing for salmon. By some accounts, Chief Seattle was among those camped there that day. David Denny was reported to have been greeted by the chief and resolved then to learn the language of the native people of the region. Low, Denny, and Terry slept near this camp their second night on Puget Sound. Two of Chief Seattle's men were hired the next day to take the men exploring. After their excursion, the men decided the gently sloping beaches of gravel and sand, surrounded by tall fir timbers on a peninsula the Indians called Smaquamox, was the place to start their settlement. Smaquamox was the southwest point of land, across Elliott Bay from Seattle's present site.

Terry, who was from New York, gave their town the name, "New York." The three men envisioned a great city at this site, as great as any on the Atlantic seaboard. Since their vision was still far in the future, the name "Alki" was suggested. This was the Chinook term for "bye-and-bye." The town then was known as "New York Alki." The name Alki remained with the peninsula after the pioneers later moved north along the bay.

Low returned to Portland to bring his family north; he brought with him a letter from David Denny to his brother, Arthur, urging him to come up as well. The two remaining men cleared the land to lay foundations for cabins. Terry and Denny notched the logs, and began to build the walls of the first log home. When Terry went in search of needed tools, David Denny stayed behind to build shelters so the families would be safe from the elements when they arrived.

Local Indians, curious as to the source of the fires, began to paddle by in canoes. Chief Seattle's daughter, Princess Angeline, paddled her canoe to see what the huge fire was all about. They were surprised to see the outline of just one log cabin in the clearing, with such an enormous fire beside it. Princess Angeline and her party were told that the land was being cleared for other settlers, and that a boatload of people was expected, including a baby. Word of the new arrivals quickly spread among the local tribes, and many of them were on shore to greet the boat when it arrived from Portland.

Unfortunately, David Denny, left alone to finish the cabin, cut his leg and became ill before the rest of the Denny party arrived. For this reason, twenty-four wet and miserable men, women, and children found themselves attempting to keep dry in a single, roofless dwelling.

After the rest of the party had arrived, the men's first order of business was to finish construction of their shelter's roof. With a new roof now over their heads, Mrs. Denny and the other women suddenly realized that Christmas was fast approaching. Although they were surrounded by evergreens and could have easily found a perfect Christmas tree, the women decided that they did not have room for a wet tree in the crowded cabin. Improvising, the ladies put a ladder against the wall and draped it with a sheet.

Christmas Eve, while the children slept, Mary and the others scoured their possessions for materials to use in making presents. The women sewed bits of lace, velvet, and ribbon into decorative collars for the little girls. The mittens and scarves the pioneer wives had knit while traveling west were pinned to the sheet so that each child had a present on Christmas morning. The party said prayers and sung hymns in celebration of the Christmas holiday. Christmas dinner consisted of a roasted goose, prepared on Mary's cookstove, and a native Northwest salmon side dish.

The first business enterprise for the new settlement was initiated by the arrival of the ship *Leonesa,* which dropped anchor off of Alki Point several months after the Denny party had settled there. The ship's captain requested the pioneers supply him with logs for market in San Francisco. In exchange for sorely needed cash and provisions, the settlers and their Indian friends began the task of logging. While the captain waited for the logs to be harvested, he entertained the women and children of the Denny party with stories of his high seas adventures. The Denny women, in turn, told tales of their adventures in crossing the plains to Oregon. When the ship had been loaded with lumber, the captain paid the settlers and Indians in provisions he could spare and the balance in cash. The settlers also placed orders for merchandise and provisions with the captain for his return voyage.

More ships followed in search of timber and exchanged compensation with the settlers and their Indian friends. The women looked forward to the conversation and provisions that the captains of the ships would bring. The ladies wondered about current fashions and complained that the clothes they had brought had become shabby and full of holes. Mary and her friends urged the captains to bring fabric with them from San Francisco on their next trip north.

One captain, upon bringing a bolt of fabric with him to Elliott Bay, bet his crew that before the ship was loaded with logs for return to California, all of the women in the settlement would be dressed alike. The captain won his bet, but as more ships ventured north to trade with the new settlement, a variety of dress material and other provisions became available. The ships became busy markets when they dropped anchor in Puget Sound, as the settlers were eager for provisions and news from the outside world.

When the new citizens of the Northwest weren't trading with docked ships, they prepared to construct a cabin for each family. Before long, many local Indian families were moving tepees onto the lots the pioneers had staked out for themselves. The Indians explained that they wanted to be close to the settlers for protection from enemy tribes. The Denny party was soon surrounded by an encampment of up to one thousand Indians who were extremely curious about their neighbors. Cultural differences caused some misunderstandings, as the natives felt free to enter the cabins and help themselves to what they found. On one occasion, an Indian man entered Mary Denny's cabin as she was frying up a large fish. As the man reached into Mary's frying pan, she was forced to defend her dinner by striking the man on the hand with a spoon.

Another custom that caused confusion was that of young Indian men placing their tepee poles so that they obstructed the doorways of the cabins. It was their custom that if a woman touched the poles to move them aside, then she must become the pole owner's wife. Several of the native men had designs on Louisa Boren. Once informed of the plan by a tribal elder who had learned Chinook (the language of trade among early trappers and various Northwest tribes) from the Hudson's Bay men, the settlers quashed the matrimonial plan. Louisa, the Sweetbriar Bride (she brought sweetbriar seeds with her from Illinois), later married David Denny in a ceremony that caused great intrigue among the local Indians.

Confrontations sometimes occurred between natives and settlers. Mary Denny, while outside the family cabin, was confronted by Nisqually Jim, who, without saying a word, leveled his rifle directly at her. He got no response from the brave pioneer woman, as she stood unflinchingly, returning his stare. He then lowered the gun and retreated. Mary's explanation for the incident was to say that, "I suppose he did it to show that he could shoot me if he wanted to."

Certainly, the new settlers to the area and the natives were not always at odds. Mary and the women of the settlement formed valuable friendships with native women who showed them how best to obtain and use the Puget Sound region's bounty of edible goods. Indian women often came to visit bearing gifts of food, such as baskets full of ripe blackberries.

After the first winter in Alki, Chief Seattle reportedly pointed out to the Denny party that the land to the northeast, sheltered within Elliott Bay, would be a more desirable location to build a town. Arthur Denny explored the area, noting the deep water harbor, which he used Mary's clothesline to measure, and nearby trail over the Cascade Mountains. In 1852, the Denny, Boren, and Bell families moved to that site, where downtown Seattle is located today. This new location provided far better shelter from the wind and winter storms.

Within the next year, many more pioneer families moved to the area. In 1853, the territorial legislature selected the name "Duwamps" for the new town, and mail was addressed to "Duwamps via Olympia, Oregon." Later, the town's name was changed to "Seattle," and after a conflict with its namesake was resolved, the name stuck and the town prospered.

In 1855, warring tribes from east of the Cascade Mountains incited violence against the settlers in the Puget Sound region. The year before, Washington Territorial Governor Issac Stevens had begun organizing treaties with Indian tribes within the territory. In exchange for cash and trinkets, the tribes were moved to reservations and their original lands were opened to settlers. In protest, some eastern Washington Indians from various tribes rebelled against prospectors and pioneers. As the warring tribes moved west, settlers in the Duwamish Valley were killed, along with two young men killed in Seattle during the fighting. Cabins were ransacked, and some burned to the ground. Mary Denny's treasured wedding dress was taken from her cabin, and she often wondered who wore it through the woods after that. The Denny families and Seattle's settlers took refuge in the old blockhouse that stood at the corner of the present-day streets of First Avenue and Cherry Street. The war, known as the Battle of Seattle, was ended rather abruptly by the presence of the warship *Decatur* in Puget Sound. When she saw the ship, Mary Denny's daughter, Louisa Catherine, remembers her mother exclaiming, "Thank God! Our prayers are answered!"

Mary and Arthur Denny became wealthy, well-respected members of Seattle society. In addition to bringing the first non-Indian baby to Seattle from Portland, Mary Ann Denny also gave birth to the second non-Indian baby, and first male child in Seattle. The baby boy, Orion Orvil, was born to them in July of 1853. The Denny's homestead fronted First Avenue and covered several present-day city blocks north to Union Street. Arthur used his civil engineering skills to survey and lay out Seattle's streets. He was instrumental in governing the young city and territory—serving in the first Territorial Legislature* and being elected as a delegate to the United States Congress. Building the city's economic foundation, Arthur helped to bring a road across the Cascades, shipping to Puget Sound, and the railroad to Seattle. Without Mary's support, Arthur would never have made the journey west.

Mary Denny was known for her benevolence—giving anonymous gifts to poor families and generously buying presents for children in need. Mary's memories kept alive the pioneer spirit. She told of making the trip between Seattle and Olympia (the nearest real

---

* The Washington Territory was officially formed from the Oregon Territory in 1853.

town) in Indian canoes, sailing vessels, steamships, trains, and auto-mobiles, and it was her ambition to make the journey by "flying machine." She recalled Secretary of the Interior William Seward vis-iting Seattle in 1869 on his way to inspect his purchase of Alaska. Seattle at that time had approximately one thousand residents, but Seward predicted future greatness for the city, calling Puget Sound "the Mediterranean of the Pacific."

Mary Ann Boren Denny passed away on December 30, 1910, at the age of eighty-eight. On the day of her death, boldface head-lines in *The Seattle Daily Times* proclaimed, "Woman Founder of City Passes Away." The article stated:

[w]ith the demise of Mrs. Denny there passed one of the oldest human landmarks in the history of the city. She was the first white woman to land on the shores of Puget Sound and together with her husband played a promi-nent part in the upbuilding of this city. Her death took from Seattle not only one of its most interesting charac-ters, but one of its noblest women. ⚜

KICK-IS-OM-LO
1811–1896

Princess Angeline—Seattle's Last Royalty

*C*oins collected by Seattle school children paid for this princess's headstone. When she died on May 31, 1896, her friends carved her a casket in the shape of a canoe. The funeral service was held at Our Lady of Good Help Cathedral, which was packed to capacity with an audience of Seattle citizens. A black hearse, drawn by matching dark horses, carried the unique coffin. The noblewoman was buried in the canoe-shaped coffin with a paddle laid across the stern. During the burial, a sprig of cedar was dropped into the grave, and local children tossed flowers atop the mound. Seattle's prominent pioneer families buried the princess in their cemetery, Lakeview Cemetery, on Capital Hill. Her grave is marked with a simple granite boulder bearing the inscription, "Princess Angeline."

Few cities in the late nineteenth century could claim an Indian princess among its citizens. A frequent sight on the streets of Seattle, this princess's crown was a red bandanna tied over wiry gray locks; the staff she carried, a bent, fire-charred, walking stick; her robe, a tattered shawl; her gowns, well-worn, calico skirts topping mismatched water-soaked shoes, if she wore any at all. The royal palace in which she lived and died was a tiny, ramshackle, wood hut on Seattle's waterfront.

Kick-Is-Om-Lo

Princess Angeline, or "Kick-Is-Om-Lo" in the language of her tribe, is believed to have been born in 1811. She was the daughter of Chief Seattle,* chief of the Suquamish, Duwamish, and six allied tribes, and namesake of the city of Seattle. The daughter of Chief Seattle's first wife, Princess Angeline told a newspaper reporter in 1891 that her father was twenty-five when she was born. She outlived three brothers and two sisters born to the chief and his second wife.

The name Angeline was bestowed upon her by her friend, Catherine Maynard, the wife of one of Seattle's more colorful pioneers, David "Doc" Maynard. When the princess was introduced to Mrs. Maynard by her married name, Kick-Is-Om-Lo Dokub Cud, Catherine Maynard replied, "Why you are much too good looking a woman to carry around such a name. I now christen you, Angeline." In her later years, she was commonly referred to as "Old Angeline," or "Princess Angeline," by the people of Seattle.

The Suquamish were one of several coastal tribes living on Puget Sound. Angeline's father, Chief Seattle, was the hereditary chief of the Suquamish Tribe who was later made chief of six allied coastal tribes for his acts of wartime bravery and skill. The people of the tribe, including young Kick-Is-Om-Lo, lived in rectangular houses made from poles, bark, and boards of cedar, with woven mats covering the doorways. The cedar roofs were each constructed with a hole to allow smoke to escape from the fires within the homes. They made clothing from deer and other animal skins which they sometimes adorned with shells and feathers. Capes and hats woven of cedar and reeds repelled the moisture from the area's frequent rain storms.

The Northwest rains nurtured a great variety of plants, wildlife, and sea creatures, giving Chief Seattle's people a wealth of choice

---

*According to Chief Seattle's son-in-law, William DeShaw, and friend, Doc Maynard, the pronunciation of the chief's name was closest to "Seattle." "Sealth" is a later interpretation.

in food. The Suquamish and Duwamish found deer, bear, cougar, and small game plentiful in the woods, an abundance of waterfowl and fish in the many freshwater lakes, and salmon and shellfish in and around Puget Sound's salty shores. Women dug for clams from the beaches and roots in the meadows and picked several types of berries. The men of these coastal tribes were known for their skill in carving cedar canoes, and the women for their weaving skills in creating baskets and clothing.

Kick-Is-Om-Lo witnessed the coming of the first white settlers to the area, beginning with the Hudson's Bay Company and settlers at Fort Nisqually near Tacoma. She and her father befriended and aided the first settlers to land on Elliott Bay. By some accounts, it was Chief Seattle who recommended to the Denny party, the first white settlers to the area, that they would have better shelter if they resided at the site of the present-day Seattle, rather than on Alki Point where they first landed. Both Chief Seattle and Princess Angeline were converted to Christianity by the early settlers.

The princess and her people showed the pioneers the bounties of the environment. On such an occasion, Angeline and her daughters took several pioneer women with them in their canoe to find the succulent blackberries growing at the water's edge. The party left the canoe tied to a rock on the shore during a low tide and ventured inland in search of berries. The women, engrossed in their harvesting of blackberries, did not notice that the tide was coming in rapidly. When they tried to return to their boat, they found it to be high tide, and their canoe was now quite a distance from the shoreline. Not only was the canoe beyond their reach, but the rock tied to the canoe was now an anchor under several feet of water.

Without saying a word, one of Angeline's daughters dashed onto the beach, removed her clothing and moccasins, and dove into the frigid waters of Puget Sound. She swam to the canoe, dove down, and retrieved the line anchoring the craft. Once the line was above water, Princess Angeline's daughter climbed into the canoe and paddled to shore to retrieve her mother and the other women.

According to legend, Princess Angeline had heard from other Indians that an attack was planned on the early pioneers' village, but she did not know exactly when this was to occur. When she heard the warriors in the woods surrounding the town signal to each other using "hooting" type sounds, Angeline knew the attackers were near and hastened to tell her settler friends. Other accounts say she paddled her canoe across Puget Sound in a raging storm to warn her friend Henry Yesler and the other settlers that the Northwest's inland and coastal tribes would soon attack. The 1856 Battle of Seattle followed.

The warship *Decatur* sailed into Elliott Bay to protect the city. Its captain, having been informed of the plan for attack, fired *Decatur's* guns into the forest at the edge of Seattle. The shot was answered by yells and gunfire from the warriors. Settlers who heard the guns rushed to the blockade at the foot of Cherry Street. The fighting ensued. Two settlers were killed, yet the number of Indian casualties was never known. According to the legend, Angeline regretted warning the settlers of the attack after her Indian lover was killed during the shelling. Two houses within the city were burned, one after looting by the warriors, the other ignited when fired upon by the ship's guns. When the fighting slowed, women and children were moved from the blockade to the ship. By morning, the warring party had gone.

Whether or not Angeline paddled her canoe across the sound to warn the settlers is disputed, but the legend contributed to her celebrity status. Yesler later denied that Angeline was responsible for warning of the attack, instead giving credit to a native man who was nicknamed Salmon Bay Curley. Mrs. Maynard maintained the legend was true.

It is, however, undisputed that in March of 1892, Angeline

marched into the Seattle Police headquarters to warn the citizens of Seattle that the world would end in June of that year. Wah-Kee-Wee-Kum, the spirit of a great medicine man, had visited her to impart this knowledge and Angeline, in her typical magnanimous spirit, decided to share this information with her white neighbors. City officials, to whom she reported her prophesy, made light of the warning by asking her if she could predict which city employee their cantankerous mayor would fire next.

As a young woman, Princess Angeline was married to Dokub Cud, a half-Cowichan chief of the Skagit Tribe. By midcentury, Dokub Cud died, leaving Angeline a widow. Angeline gave birth to two daughters, Betsy and Mary, both of whom married white settlers. Mary wed William De Shaw, a respected, local merchant. De Shaw accumulated wealth through a variety of enterprises, including smoking salmon for market. No doubt, Mary enjoyed a better life than that of her sister.

Daughter Betsy suffered much abuse from her mean-spirited, alcoholic husband. As a way of escaping this abuse, Betsy hanged herself with a red bandanna tied to a beam in a shed on Commercial Street. Angeline discovered the body of her daughter hanging from the rafters of her cabin, her baby boy wailing in a basket at her feet. Betsy's infant son, Joe Foster, went to live with his grandmother. Angeline raised the child with love, but he took after his father. He was always in trouble, frequently in jail, and he caused her much grief.

It was a common sight to see Angeline sitting on city sidewalks, hawking her wares. Angeline sold clams and baskets on the streets of Seattle and moccasins to people arriving in ships at the waterfront piers. She also did wash for many of Seattle's founding families. These tasks would have afforded her a comfortable living had she not spent most of her earnings posting bail and paying fines for her wayward grandson, Joe Foster.

A favorite subject for visiting journalists and photographers, her fame spread, and Angeline was invited to tour the world with George Francis Train in his quest to promote the Northwest. After a purse of several thousand dollars was raised for her fare, a delegation of local citizens visited her to propose the promotional trip. The delegates were dumbfounded when the princess flatly refused their offer. She explained that her revered father (whom she called "Hy-as Ty-ee," or "Great Father") would be so angry at her for running off with a crazy man that he would turn in his grave.

Carnival operators and dime museum owners also offered Angeline money to travel with them as she became known nationwide. Aiding in the spread of her fame were souvenir spoons and dishes bearing her likeness which were sold to tourists. Though she would not hear of leaving her home, and she refused to be displayed in such a manner, Angeline did enjoy being shown off as a local celebrity and became the most photographed face in the city, although no photos of her as a young woman exist. Never wishing to leave Seattle, she expressed a desire to be buried with her pioneer friends, or "tillicums."

The farthest Angeline ever traveled from home was on a trip to Olympia with her famous father to protest the naming of the city after the great chief. The law among the Duwamish and Suquamish tribes was that when a person died, his name was not to be spoken aloud for five years. If the deceased was a chief, the silence was observed for ten years. When the name was passed on to a son, this law became moot. Should the tradition not be observed, the dead chief would roll over in his grave every time his name was spoken. Chief Seattle was horrified when the founding fathers proposed naming the city after him. Wishing to avoid a terrible fate, he took his entire family to Olympia to ask the governor to intercede. The governor was eventually able to convince Seattle that his last sleep would be peaceful. Reportedly, the chief was ultimately pleased with the honor.

On May 6, 1891, President Benjamin Harrison arrived for an official visit to Seattle, and the people of Seattle did their best to honor the occasion despite a torrential rainstorm. Angeline was presented to the President as the daughter of Chief Seattle and the head of her nation. Although she understood English, she always spoke in the Chinook jargon (the common language of traders and the various Northwest tribes). The princess shook President Harrison's hand, curtsied, and greeted him, "Kla-how-ya,"

"Hello, how are you?" the usually staid head of state responded politely in turn.

As she aged, Angeline became quick tempered and sensitive to insult. Often teased by the local boys, she carried rocks in her skirt pockets which she tossed with great accuracy to ward off such attacks.

One pioneer woman recounted her experience with the wrath of Angeline. After moving to Seattle in 1880, she and Angeline had become friends. Angeline frequently visited her home, always bringing freshly dug clams with her. On one occasion, the young mother was strolling the city streets with her small daughter and pushing her baby in a buggy. Not seeing Angeline sitting on the sidewalk, she rolled the wheels of the stroller over Angeline's toes. Angeline leapt to her feet and began to curse profusely at the startled woman. No apology would do, and from that day on whenever the woman encountered Angeline on the streets of Seattle, Angeline would point to her foot and proceed to swear at the embarrassed lady. The most hurtful thing for the pioneer woman was that Angeline never again returned to her home for a friendly visit.

The early Seattleites owed their lives to Chief Seattle and his people. Perhaps they looked after Angeline in her later years because they felt responsible for her fate. Although this woman of noble birth lived her later years emersed in the white man's world, she always seemed out of place in the bustling "modern" city.

Angeline's needs were simple; she never took anything she did not need. If she had extras, she "potlatched" the item, or gave it away in the Indian manner. After she could no longer dig clams, gather firewood, or work for a living, the charity of the early settlers kept her going. When she needed shelter, Henry Yesler donated lumber from his mill to build the princess a waterfront cabin.

At the onset of her illness, her well-meaning, pioneer friends placed her in Seattle General Hospital. Angeline railed against being taken from her simple home and placed in what she deemed a jail. After much wailing and thrashing about, she was returned to her cabin, where she died on May 31, 1896. A black crêpe drape was hung across her doorway on the day of her death.

When she died at the estimated age of eighty-five, the population of Seattle was more than 60,000. Angeline had witnessed the growth of her small Indian village into a log-cabin settlement; and, by the end of her life, the land over which her father once reigned had become a thriving metropolis. ❧

MOTHER JOSEPH
1823–1902

Chief of the Lady Black Robes

Clouds of dust erupted as the stagecoach wheels ground to a halt on the narrow mountain road. Four masked gunmen greeted the startled passengers with the cold steel barrels of their revolvers. "Get out of the stage, and throw your bags to the side of the road! Now!" barked the gang leader. Pistols were trained on the terrified travelers as they disembarked. A middle aged nun among the passengers whispered to the others, "Pray, pray!"

Once the luggage had been deposited by the roadside, the people were herded back into the stagecoach as the robbers began to rifle through the baggage. The nun looked up from her praying as if seized by a sudden impulse. She jumped to her feet and called out, "Mister . . . Mister . . ." Her co-passengers, thinking they might all be killed any minute, urged to her to be quiet.

The sister was undaunted and spoke more authoritatively, addressing the youngest member of the gang with a thick French accent, "Mister . . . my boy." The young thief started, as if no one had ever spoken to him in such a manner. For a moment, he stopped his pilfering.

"My boy, please give me that black bag!"

Mother Joseph

While the other passengers, cowering in the stage, looked on in horror, the young man asked, "Which?"

"That one—the black one over there."

The boy searched through the pile of luggage, then held one up with a questioning look toward the sister.

"No, no."

He continued to sort through the bags, eventually coming upon a large carpetbag, and held it up for the nun's approval.

"Yes, my man. Give it to me. There is nothing in it you would want."

Stunned by the nun's audacity, the bandit brought her the bag.

"Thank you. God bless you," commended the sister graciously. The boy then returned to looting with his gang, and the nun re-joined her companions in the stage. She winked at the petrified young nun traveling with her and patted her bag. Several hundred dollars the sisters had collected that day from miners had been saved from the bandits.

The two nuns, Sister Mary Augustine and her bold superior, Mother Joseph of the Sacred Heart, continued on this begging tour through the mines of Oregon, Idaho, and Colorado for another sixteen months. The Sisters of Providence sought contributions from generous miners to fund the building of an orphanage in Vancouver, Washington Territory. The stagecoach robbery was but one of many adventures and hardships that Mother Joseph endured while on her begging tours throughout the West to raise money for her charitable endeavors.

* * *

She was born Esther Pariseau in French-speaking Saint Elzear, Quebec, on April 16, 1823. Esther was the third of twelve children of Joseph and Francoise Pariseau. During the snowy winter months when he could not farm, Joseph Pariseau worked as a coach maker, a talent he became well known for throughout the region. As a young girl, Esther worked beside her father in his shop, learning to love the tools and wood crafting at which her father was so skilled.

Madame Pariseau, educated by the Sisters of Notre Dame in Montreal, taught her children to read and write. When she was seventeen, Esther entered the Saint Martin de Laval boarding school run by Mademoiselle Elizabeth Bruyere in 1840. Strong and direct, Esther had a dignified presence and a natural capacity for organization and leadership. She loved school and adored her instructor, Mademoiselle Bruyere, but it did not surprise Esther when her teacher announced she was leaving the school to become a nun.

Shortly after her instructor left, Esther felt her own calling. She was inspired to work for the poor and infirm by a visit from Monseigneur Bourget to her family's farm. Father Bourget told of a new order of nuns, the Sisters of Providence, who were serving the poor with wonderful works of charity for the sick and destitute in Montreal. The priest sought money to construct a convent, the Asile of Providence, for the new order of nuns.

Joseph Pariseau brought his young daughter to this newly built convent, the Asile, on December 26, 1843. As Joseph respectfully approached the dignified Mother Superior Gamelin, he stated his purpose and introduced his daughter.

> Madame, my daughter, Esther, wishes to dedicate herself to the religious life. She is now twenty years of age, and for some time she has prayed with the family for enlightenment as to the decision she is about to make. . . It is a great sacrifice for me to part with Esther, but if you will accept her into your company, she will be a real acquisition. She has had all the education that her mother and I could give her, besides what the Parish school could of-

Black Robes on a begging tour.

fer. My daughter can read, write, figure accurately, sew, cook, spin, and do all manner of housework. She can even do carpentering, handle a hammer and saw as well as her father. She can also plan for others, and succeeds in all she undertakes. I assure you, Madame, she will make a good superior some day.

Esther cried out in embarrassment, "Oh, Father, please! *Pour l'amour de Mon Dieu!* Must you tell all my accomplishments, my talents, and the work my mother taught me?"

"Let your father speak, child," interrupted the mother superior, "What he says interests me very much."

Joseph continued, "Only twenty now, Esther is healthy and

strong, has never been ill. She is clever and knows her mind. She is very well determined to give herself to God in the Providence to answer the appeal of Monseigneur Bourget for helpers."

"And you, Monsieur Pariseau, are you willing to make the sacrifice of your daughter?"

"Certainly, Madame, that is why I brought her today. This is her Christmas offering to the Divine Child, the gift of herself."

After arranging Esther's dowry and a hug goodbye, Joseph was gone. Esther now entered into a new life. She took her vows in 1845, and with them the name Sister Joseph in honor of her father.

When, in April of 1852, Father Francis Norbert Blanchet (Archbishop of Oregon City) and his brother, Father Magloire Blanchet (Bishop of Nisqually) visited the Asile, the direction of Sister Joseph's life changed again. Father Magloire Blanchet had spent six years in a remote wilderness called the "Oregon Territory," most recently as the Bishop of the Nisqually Diocese. Father Francis Norbert Blanchet had been in the territory since 1838. All at the Asile were intrigued with tales of the Oregon Territory, including Sister Joseph, who had dreams of going west and working with native people.

The Fathers Blanchet had been well received by the Hudson's Bay Company, the entity that controlled the Oregon/Washington Territory for Great Britain. The Hudson's Bay enclave, Fort Vancouver was the dominant settlement in the Washington Territory at that time. Catholics were welcomed by Dr. McLoughlin, the head of the Hudson's Bay Company, and the trappers who were mostly Catholic. The priests had a huge job in covering all of this territory and were in need of sisters to help them. Upon this return to the Asile in 1852, the Bishop of Nisqually spoke of this need for sisters to serve in the new land. Sister Joseph volunteered, but the council in Montreal refused to let her go, as she was much needed there.

In November of 1856, after a previous expedition of nuns

had failed, Sister Joseph was allowed to be part of a new expedition. Frightened and confused by the wild country, winter storms, and floods, the first group of nuns had sailed for home, only to end up settling in Chile. The new party of five mostly French-speaking nuns was led by Father Magloire Blanchet. The priest appointed Sister Joseph as their mother superior, a job she reluctantly accepted. She was given the title, "Sister Joseph of the Sacred Heart."

Due to strong anti-Catholic sentiments of the time, the nuns were advised not to wear their habits when traveling, especially not in New York City, where they were to embark upon their journey. Having borrowed and purchased used clothing for their travels, the women, in their unfashionable attire, attracted far more attention than a few habits would have drawn. While riding cabs through the streets of the city they heard cries such as, "Look at the Quaker ladies!" The waiters at the Catholic-owned hotel where they stayed, could hardly contain their laughter when the women first entered their dining room. Following dinner, the maitre d' tipped the sisters that they had nothing to fear were they to wear their habits in the hotel, on the boats, or even in the city itself. The sisters must have breathed a collective sigh of relief. From this time on, Mother Joseph was never without her habit.

On November 6, 1856, the party sailed from New York to Panama, where they crossed the Isthmus of Panama by train. The sisters were lucky to have a train in 1855, as the expedition of nuns in 1852 had crossed Panama on mules. Even so, this train ride of forty-seven miles took them five hours.

Once at the Pacific Ocean, the nuns boarded a ship to San Francisco. Then, after a few days rest, transferred to a steamer bound for Vancouver. This was to be the hardest part of the trip. Winter storms made for turbulent seas. Ferocious waves tossed the ship like a toy boat, and trunks and baggage were thrown about by the violent lurching of the boat. Everything not tied down flew around the cabins as the vessel creaked and groaned. The main mast was blown over. It was impossible for the passengers to leave their bunks, as they could not stand without being heaved through the air. The nuns were chilled to the bone and sea sick—so much so that Mother Joseph thought she might die.

When the seas finally calmed, the Captain announced they were entering a place known as "The Grave Yard," due to its hidden shoals and shifting sands. Many ships had been lost crossing the sandbars at the mouth of the Columbia River. Landing safely at Astoria, Oregon, they traveled on the Columbia to Vancouver.

Along the Columbia, the nuns saw dense forests with trees so tall they disappeared into the fog. They saw little civilization, but for a few log cabins. At Fort Vancouver, the party was greeted by a small crowd of what seemed to be all young soldiers. Fort Vancouver, once run by the British Hudson's Bay Company, was now an American military post where there were only a few women and no Indians.

At the Vancouver Mission, the women found no housing and a priest who opposed their staying at Vancouver. Vicar General Brouillet thought it more appropriate that the sisters reside in Olympia, the new capital of the Washington Territory. The Vicar argued with Bishop Blanchet that the women would be better provided for in Olympia. Here they had only a shed to give them for quarters. Mother Joseph, overhearing the conversation, offered to stay in the shed.

The nuns spent their first night in Father Blanchet's dusty attic, which they first had to clean! Their bedding consisted of dirty old quilts used by settlers and Indians who took refuge at the mission during the Indian Wars. The following months were also spent with Father Blanchet, crowded into his simple board house over which the nuns assumed care. Mother Joseph constructed a dormitory-refectory-community room. Using the skills acquired from her father, she built bunk beds, a table hinged to the wall, and cupboards.

The sisters spent the unfamiliar rainy winter planning for a convent and a school. On Ash Wednesday, February 22, 1857, the nuns moved to their own small, wood frame house. In it Mother Joseph had constructed an attic dormitory and chapel complete with an altar and tabernacle.

Prior to the school's opening, the nuns received their first little pupil. Three-year-old Emily Lake arrived at the convent with a mother eager to leave her behind with the nuns. The child was fatherless, of mixed race, and appeared dirty and neglected. Mother Joseph was delighted to take the girl; she held the tiny, grimy hand tightly and assured the mother they would care for Emily. The mother showed no emotion, just relief, and made a quick exit, never to be seen again. Mother Joseph adored little Emily, and for the first time in her life, Emily was wanted and protected. She could often be seen following Mother Joseph around in the garden and in the chapel.

Before long, a baby boy named William was placed with the sisters. Mother Joseph pitied the little orphans, often placed with guardians who mistreated them and raised them without morals. Such guardians sometimes traveled hundreds of miles to the mission to abandon these poor children.

Next, an eighty-five-year-old man, feeble and poor, asked to be taken in. There was so little room at the tiny convent that the old man's bed was put next to the stove in the kitchen.

On April 15, 1857, the first Catholic school in the Northwest opened its doors to seven little girls. The school was small and plain, but impeccably clean. A language barrier impeded the teaching of these American pupils as only two of the nuns spoke English. Mother Joseph, who spoke very little English, often wrote to her mother superior in Montreal of the need for more English-speaking nuns. She particularly hoped that the mother superior might send a music teacher west.

Mother Joseph found Vancouver to be a town full of sin. She

was aghast at the lifestyles of her fellow French Canadians. In her letters to her mother superior, she noted Vancouver's population is a mixture of people from everywhere. Both the Catholics and Protestants have been poorly schooled in religion, although the Protestants welcomed religious instruction for their children.

Initially, the sisters' mission was to create schools and orphanages. Mother Joseph had hoped to work and live among Indian people but, to her dismay, she learned that "these poor unfortunates" had been driven to the mountains by an increasing number of white settlers. She longed to establish Indians schools, but the Indian Wars of the mid-1800s made for turbulent times. Bishop Blanchet, on occasion, brought orphaned Indian children to the convent from east of the Cascade Mountains.

From the time they arrived, the sisters had visited Vancouver's sick and infirm. In the spring of 1858, they were called to take in a young man named John Lloyd who was afflicted with tuberculosis. Though they wanted to help the poor, sick, homeless man, they had no place to house him. The vicar proposed building a hospital. The ladies of the town—Catholic, Protestant, and Jewish alike—assembled to assist in the endeavor.

Mother Joseph had built a tiny clapboard cabin which she intended to be used for a laundry and bakery. The town's ladies offered to complete the interior and furnish the small building if Mother Joseph would allow them to use it as their hospital. Mother Joseph agreed, and Saint Joseph's, the first hospital in the Northwest, opened in April of 1858, with only four beds. Before long, young John, the waiting patient, was admitted to Saint Joseph's and was soon followed by many sick and injured Northwesterners. Thus, the nuns had created the first official school, orphanage, and hospital in the Northwest.

In the spring of 1861, a mentally ill woman was placed in the sisters' care. They then devoted two small buildings to housing the "mentally deranged." By 1866, there were twenty-five patients cared for under a contract with the Washington Territory. The patients later moved to a more spacious house, but when the territorial government revoked their contract to care for the insane over a dispute resulting from Mother Joseph's insistence on being paid in gold coin rather than "greenbacks," the home to Saint John of God Asylum, became the new Saint Joseph's Hospital.

At the urging of priests, the sisters founded Saint Vincents in Portland, Oregon, in 1875 and Providence Hospital in Seattle in 1877. These were the first of twenty-nine institutions Mother Joseph established during her forty-six years in the Pacific Northwest. Although high mortality rates in the logging camps around Seattle were creating an urgent need for hospitals, the sisters often met with less than enthusiastic welcomes from the citizens they came to serve. At the time, Seattle was a rough, muddy, sparsely populated, Protestant or atheist, logging and seaport town. The people were suspicious of the French speaking nuns and of Catholics in general. However, the sisters persisted, and the people came to depend upon them.

In 1881, after the hospital had outgrown two buildings, Mother Joseph designed a new elaborate Providence Hospital in Seattle. This stately building was like nothing the city had ever seen, with its gas-lighting system and steam-driven elevators. Mother Joseph conducted the final inspection of Providence Hospital in a sawdust-covered habit with her hammer swinging from her tool belt.

Although Mother Joseph's first preference was to work with a hammer and saw, she saw the need to raise money to build and run these institutions. Asking for financial support from the community flew in the face of tradition, but the industrious sister would do what was necessary to get the job done and then later pray for forgiveness. Mother Joseph and her nuns traveled on begging tours throughout the West, appealing to miners to fund their charitable works. To Westerners they were known as the "Lady Black Robes," with Mother Joseph designated, by the Indians, as their chief.

Mother Joseph's description of one such begging tour can be found in the annals of the Sisters of Providence for July of 1866. Mother Joseph and Sister Catherine had traveled by boat to Wallula, near Walla Walla, and then by stagecoach to Walla Walla and on to Idaho City where they collected three thousand dollars from the miners. During their six-week begging tour in Idaho, they met with varied reactions from those they appealed to for alms. In Idaho City, the nuns were received cordially even by, "infidels and Protestants who marveled at [their] daring, and commended [their] perseverance." Often in the mining camps the sisters encountered cold indifference, and even abuse. In her habit, Mother Joseph made perilous descents into the black mines, hundreds of feet below the earth's surface, in order to contact the many miners who worked underground.

Encouraged by good fortune in Idaho, the two nuns set out for Montana. The miners of Montana were not as enthusiastic as those in Idaho, yet the sisters still collected two thousand dollars. Following a visit with four, lonely sisters at the Saint Ignatius Mission forty miles north of Missoula, the women set off for home on horseback. They would no longer have the luxury of traveling by boat or stagecoach. Only on horseback could they pass through the forests that lay between them and the lower Columbia country. The sisters at Saint Ignatius loaned them saddles and riding habits—the Jesuit Fathers provided the horses.

"In the last days of September our little caravan set out. It was composed of Father Louis Saint-Onge, an Indian named Sapiel from the mission, Father Joseph Giorda, S.J., who went with us as far as Missoula, Sister Catherine and myself." With them were two pack horses with provisions and a tent. They traveled through dark forests and steep, precipitous mountains on narrow Indian trails. Except for some lone miners, the party met no one.

Every evening they looked for a clearing, with water and grass for the animals, in which to make camp. Father Saint-Onge hunted for game, Sapiel cared for the horses and collected firewood, and the sisters took charge of cooking crêpes and fresh meat. They ate, conversed, sang hymns, and prayed before the light of the fire. In preparation for bed, they pitched their tent, wrapped themselves in blankets, and with saddles for pillows, retired for the night.

One day while riding on steep Rocky Mountain trails, a fierce storm broke upon them. Low, dark clouds hung overhead menacingly. When the clouds broke, the gradually increasing rainstorm gave way to a relentless downpour, thunder, and lightning. Traveling in the deep mud was challenging, as was building a fire in the driving rain. By the time camp was set up, all were soaked to the skin. With great difficulty, Sapiel was able to set a small fire inside the tent. They lay down that night in the mud, as near to the fire as possible. Several nights later, an enormous tree fell just three feet from the tent in which the two nuns were sleeping.

Traveling through dense forests over an animal trail, they would often lose sight of each other on the winding paths. On the ninth day of travel, the party, overcome with fatigue, camped in a ravine between two mountain ranges. They were jolted awake by a terrifying howl which, according to Mother Joseph's account, "froze the blood in our veins." Sapiel quickly cut wood and circled the camp with fire, since wolves do not ordinarily cross a line of fire. Soon the woods were full of the horrible howls. The travelers knew wolves, which hunt in packs, were now all around them. The horses, tethered inside the ring of fire, were lathered to a frenzy. Trees surrounding the area had been dried by a prior fire, and soon the flames, meant to protect the party, were a serious threat to their safety. Branches and brush around them began to burn, embers cracked and popped menacingly, and great limbs burned and crashed to the ground. The whole night was spent battling burning cinders and blinding smoke, while surrounded by an increasing number of howling wolves. Some provisions were destroyed, the tent had caught fire several times, and the saddles were singed. The dawn's light chased away the wolves, ending a night of trauma and prayer. Exhausted, they fell to the ground with fatigue.

Suddenly, a new sound was heard, that of horses tramping up the trail. Before they could react, a party of Indian warriors with painted faces surrounded the camp. The Indian braves noticed the crosses around their necks and recognized Father Saint-Onge. They immediately offered hand signs of friendship and respect. The Indian people were drawn to Catholicism, the long, dark robes of the priests and nuns, and the symbols of the faith. They trusted the priests far more than the rugged frontiersmen they met in the territory, and the priests often acted as envoys between the tribes and the settlers. The party shared a meal with the Indians, but "cringed before the scalping knives" that hung at their sides.

Another evening while still in the Coeur d'Alene forests of Idaho, Father Saint-Onge spotted tracks while raising the tent. Sapiel identified the tracks as those of a grizzly bear, known to his people as the most dangerous creature in the forest. The only arms the men had against the massive beast were a six-shooter and an ax. The two did not mention the danger to the others, and the night passed without incident.

Early the next morning, Sapiel went to check on the horses. He was horrified to find an enormous grizzly bear attacking one of the horses. The bear, spying Sapiel, jumped the log corral and made straight for him. Sapiel took off running with the grizzly in close pursuit. The bear's claws swiped at the man several times, and he could hear teeth grinding near his head. Sapiel somehow managed to elude the creature's great claws. Suddenly, the bear became distracted by the sound of tinkling bells. A pack train of mules came into sight and the cries of the Mexicans leading the mules, and those of Father Saint-Onge, scared the grizzly off.

"One more adventure before the curtain falls on this unforgettable tour of the Rocky Mountains," Mother Joseph wrote in her chronicles. On a quiet night on the trail, Father Saint-Onge, sleeping under the stars, was awakened by a sensation of something cold gliding up his trouser leg. He knew it was a rattlesnake. With extreme will power he lay perfectly still so that the reptile would go to sleep near the warmth of his body. After several minutes, which must have seemed an eternity, Father bound to his feet so that the serpent slid away from him. The snake was seen slinking away leaving the poor priest shaken, but unscathed.

The weary travelers arrived back in Vancouver on October 16, 1866, exhausted by the long horseback journey fraught with dangers. The sisters were grateful for the financial success of their tour and for their safe return home.

Many years of contention between the United States and the British Hudson's Bay Company put the sisters' property claim in Vancouver in jeopardy. In 1869, the American government served the mission with an eviction notice, which was later rescinded under protest by the Bishop.

Mother Joseph saw that it was time to consolidate all of their scattered little buildings. Her dream was to construct a magnificent brick convent. With the help of the Bishop's nephew, Mother Joseph negotiated with local businesses for building materials. The nun had developed a reputation as a force with which to be reckoned, even among seasoned salesmen. She could not be pushed around by businessmen who sometimes saw the nuns' works as encroachment and their free labor as unfair competition. It was unusual at the time to find a woman with such will and determination. Her blunt, direct manner sometimes made her seem difficult, even among the sisters.

Mother Joseph's strong work ethic and love of construction made her a task master. She was known to rip apart faulty construction with her own hands, only to rebuild the structures herself. Witnesses recall the black-habited Mother Joseph emerging from beneath a building after checking its foundation, or balancing on a high beam to test its strength. Stories grew of her skill as a carver and woodworker. Many of the convent's statues were carved by Mother Joseph herself.

In 1874, Mother Joseph moved the sisters, the boarders, and the orphans into the House of Providence on Tenth and Reserve Streets in Vancouver. The people of the Pacific Coast cities were amazed at the enormity of the convent, unlike any structure then found in Washington or Oregon. The sisters now had their grand convent; however, they also were in debt twenty thousand dollars. Once again Mother Joseph set out on a begging tour, this time to the Frasier River country of Canada, raising ten thousand dollars, in just three weeks.

For nearly forty-seven years, Mother Joseph of the Sacred Heart continued her work throughout the Northwest. She built schools for Indian children at Tulalip, Colville, and Coeur d'Alene, along with dozens of hospitals and orphanages. Even at age seventy-seven, she answered a call to build an orphanage in British Columbia.

In her last years, Mother Joseph was nearly blinded by a brain tumor and mostly confined to the convent. She died January 19, 1902, of her condition. Her dying words were to remind the sisters to always attend to the care of the poor without regret.

In 1980, the state of Washington named Mother Joseph its most distinguished citizen. A bronze statue of the nun, hammer by her side, was constructed by Felix de Weldon for the Statuary Hall of the House of Representatives in Washington, D.C. Mother Joseph was only the fifth woman, first Catholic nun, and second Washingtonian (joining Dr. Marcus Whitman) to be so honored. Today, the West Coast Lumberman's Association acknowledges Mother Joseph as the first (non-Indian) Northwestern artist to work in the medium of wood. The American Institute of Architects named Mother Joseph the Pacific Northwest's first architect in 1953, fifty-one years after her death. In addition to her wonderful work on behalf of the poor, building schools, hospitals and orphanages, she designed architecture far ahead of anything in the West at the time. ❧

Mercer Girl

$\mathcal{A}$ large, restless crowd, comprised mostly of men, met the ship as it docked in Elliott Bay. The air was thick with excitement and anticipation. Seattle's large population of single men, who outnumbered the women ten to one, eagerly awaited the arrival of Asa Mercer and his "Mercer Girls."

At the urging of local businessmen, Asa Mercer had ventured east in search of eligible women willing to relocate to the untamed Pacific Northwest. Asa Shinn Mercer, the twenty-three-year-old president of the Territorial University (now known as the University of Washington), saw a solution to the problem of the Northwest's dearth of eligible females and the abundance of lonely bachelors. On the East Coast, the situation was reversed. The Civil War had decimated the population of young men, and young women were faced with bleak prospects regarding marriage and employment.

Though not the first to see the solution, Mercer became the first to act on the idea of importing New England's women to the Pacific Northwest. He approached the territorial governor, Pickering, and the Territorial Legislature. Although they liked the plan, they could not approve funding, as the territory was not wealthy. Instead,

Lizzie Ordway

Mercer collected enough money from individual businessmen to fund a trip to Boston to act upon his plan.

In Boston, Mercer advertised the virtues of Puget Sound and met with interested groups of women—many war widows and orphans. He detailed the charms of the region and the vast opportunities for employment in this new frontier where women were at a premium. An example of one such enticing speech follows:

> The climate of Washington Territory is marked by two seasons only, winter and summer. From the first day of April until the middle of November no other spot on this green earth boasts such a mild, equitable and delightful climate as does the valley of Puget Sound. Refreshing showers visit us every few weeks and all nature breathes of purity and healthfulness.

Mercer offered to lead the most worthy candidates to this wonderful new land. Receiving a stack of applications, he chose only women who were of the highest caliber in community standing, education, and moral character. From this choice group, he limited his candidates to those with enough courage and pioneer spirit to brave a long journey to the other end of the continent with virtually no chance of returning home.

In the end, eleven chosen women joined Mercer as he sailed west. Asa Mercer promised the women that they would find careers in the Northwest; he said nothing about marriage. He kept his word, finding mostly teaching positions for them in Seattle and outlying towns.

The party of twelve left New York aboard a steamer, traveled by train across the Isthmus of Panama, took a steamer from Panama City to San Francisco, before traveling by lumber bark from San

Francisco to Port Gamble, and sloop from Port Gamble to Seattle. The sloop *Kidder* arrived in Seattle at midnight, on May 16, 1864. Seattle, expecting the party, was awake to see them land. Carrying lanterns, curious women and respectful young bachelors—washed, combed, and in their newest and cleanest clothes—met the *Kidder* as it docked on Yesler's Wharf.

The arrival of the eleven potential brides from the East on May 16, 1864, was a monumental event in Seattle. Every single man who could afford to purchase a new suit did so; those that could not bought new overalls. All eligible men were on the dock when the ship arrived. Asa Mercer greeted the men, telling them that these women were of the finest caliber and that if these men desired wives, they must court them in the customary manner. A grand celebration was held in honor of the women. The party lasted from the moment the first passenger walked down the gangplank to well into the early morning hours. A reception was held the next day in the town hall, with the festive mood continuing on through the week.

This first expedition was a success and, as a result, Asa S. Mercer was elected to the Territorial Legislature. Two years later, he made a second trip east with the dream of enticing five hundred women to Seattle. Mercer met with many obstacles and, in the end, only twenty-eight single women landed on Yesler's Wharf.

These refined women left the comforts of modern society in the East for the rugged Pacific Northwest in order to bring New England's culture and refinement to the Northwest. Some were likely lured west by romantic ideas of adventure on a new frontier. The "Mercer Girls" were treated hospitably by Seattleites, who took them into their homes to live until they either married or found employment as milliners, dressmakers, or teachers (the occupations available to women of the day).

Within a year of their arrival, all of the Mercer Girls* remaining in the Northwest had married, except one—thirty-six-year-old Elizabeth "Lizzie" M. Ordway. Miss Ordway never had any intention of marrying at the end of her voyage. Rather, as one of Washington's first career women, Lizzie's goal was, "to carry the educational standards of New England to the new community beyond the Rockies."

* * *

The eldest child of a wealthy family, Elizabeth M. Ordway was born July 4, 1828, in Lowell, Massachusetts. Enoch Ordway, Lizzie's father, ran a business which imported cotton. A witty conversant with considerable charm, Lizzie moved in high society circles and was a sought-after party guest, although her advanced views were seen as unconventional for the time.

Graduating from the prestigious Ipswich Academy, Lizzie earned a certificate in ancient and modern languages. She was fluent in five modern tongues and knowledgeable about Greek and Roman language and culture. A major influence on Lizzie at the Ipswich Academy was her teacher Gail Hamilton, who wrote under the pen name Mary Abigail Dodge. Hamilton was a noted feminist and author. This influence cultivated Lizzie's feminism and sharpened her skills at bantering with wit and humor. Lizzie was strong in her convictions, very decisive, and willing to act on the strength of her own judgment. Following her graduation from the Academy, Miss Ordway taught school in Lowell, Massachusetts, for twelve years.

In Seattle, Lizzie's first home was with pioneer Henry Yesler and his family, where she and Sarah Yesler concurred on the goals of the suffrage movement—providing equal rights and voting privileges to women. Four months after her arrival, when a fellow Mer-

---

*One of the Mercer girls died on Whidbey Island, where she taught school, and another returned to Lowell, Massachusetts.

cer Girl—who was the teacher at Whidbey Island's school—died unexpectedly, Lizzie was asked to take the helm of the school. She moved across Puget Sound to Whidbey Island and taught in Coupeville for the remainder of the 1864 school year.

In 1866, Miss Ordway took command of the Port Madison school on the Kitsap Peninsula. From 1866 until her death in 1897, she was identified as a leader in education for Kitsap County.

Port Madison vied with Seattle as a commercial port in the late nineteenth century due to the extensive lumber business on the peninsula. Mill towns were known for their rough atmosphere, with their schools being no different. Into this environment came the petite, well-bred lady from New England. A tiny, slender, light-haired woman with steel gray eyes, Miss Ordway soon had control of the tough Port Madison school.

Miss Lizzie possessed a pioneer spirit in teaching rough-hewn students under rugged, primitive conditions. Surrounded by the wild Northwestern woods and enduring isolation and solitude, coarse characters, and apathetic students, she persevered. Without roads, many students paddled to school in canoes or walked along beaches to the schoolhouses. The dangerous Puget Sound currents occasionally caused small vessels to capsize and since some children had drowned in this manner, teachers were advised to watch the tides and dismiss class only when the tides favored water travel.

When Miss Ordway started a school in Port Orchard, the district was the wildest and most unsettled on the Kitsap Peninsula. Teachers were advised against living alone in the "teacherage," or living quarters adjacent to the schoolhouse. A young girl lived with Lizzie and cared for the house while Lizzie was teaching. Lizzie tutored the young girl in the evenings in turn.

As a result of her achievements in Port Madison, Lizzie Ordway was recruited to Seattle to start the city's first public school. Prior to this, Seattle's young had been educated in private, tuition-based classes held in homes, churches, and the University building. Seattle now had a population of twelve hundred citizens who thought more formal education for their children was in order. Together they purchased land and erected a two-story, wood-framed schoolhouse fronting on Third Avenue between Madison and Spring Streets. In August of 1870, Miss Ordway opened Seattle School District Number 1, as the first principal and teacher. The first morning at the new Central School, 125 children showed up in front of one teacher. After welcoming them all warmly, she regretfully told her classroom full of eager faces that she would not be able to keep them all. Then, she sent the youngest would-be pupils home, "to wait a while and to ripen a little." The new teacher reprimanded Seattle's citizens for their lack of forethought. By the second week of school, a second teacher had been hired. Miss Ordway taught at the Central School until she was, once again, summoned to Kitsap County.

Kitsap County officials implored Miss Lizzie to return. She taught again in Port Madison, and later in the towns of Port Blakely and Port Orchard. She was uprooted from her position in Port Orchard when district officials needed help with unruly students in Port Gamble, another rough and tumble mill town. She won over her classes in Port Gamble, commanding respect and admiration from students and their parents. Of this experience she wrote:

> I was sent for to take charge of the school, but, hesitated to do so because its reputation had been that of a school hard to manage. I need not say that I have been agreeably disappointed. The pupils seem to come readily under discipline and I hope I have succeeded in rousing an ambition to redeem themselves, and to feel a love for and an interest in their studies. They have numbered during the past year 39, with an average attendance of 30.

She was remembered by one student at Port Gamble as being, "very small, like a bit of Dresden china, and always beautifully dressed. She made you think of lavender and old lace." The students also knew that Miss Lizzie would not hesitate to use a switch when necessary. Known as a strict disciplinarian, she demanded perfection from her pupils and received it in return.

Elizabeth Ordway believed in women's rights and was deeply involved in the suffrage movement. She served as secretary of the Washington Women's Suffrage Organization. In that capacity, she hosted Susan B. Anthony and Oregon's Abigail Scott Duniway when they visited Washington to lobby the territorial legislature of 1871 for the women's vote. As an officer, she joined Susan B. Anthony on the platform when Miss Anthony addressed Seattle on the suffrage movement. In their fight for the vote and equal rights for women, the suffragettes endured criticism and ridicule from the local male population, as well as the press.

Washington's suffrage bill, which Lizzie Ordway had lobbied for so heartily, was defeated in 1871. In 1883, the Washington Legislature granted the vote to women, but the bill was repealed a few years later in 1887 when the territorial supreme court ruled the law unconstitutional. Washington women were permanently awarded the right to vote in 1910.

Beaten in spirit, Miss Ordway left Washington in 1872, accepting a job at a private girls' school in San Francisco. The climate of San Francisco was not to her liking, so Miss Lizzie returned to her hometown of Lowell, Massachusetts.

The delicate lady from New England now had the Northwest in her blood and after a few months, she returned to the Kitsap Peninsula to teach in Port Madison and in another untamed mill town, Port Blakely. After five years as Port Blakely's teacher, at the urging of local citizens, L. M. Ordway ran for the position of Superintendent of Schools for Kitsap County. As L. M. Ordway, using initials to disguise her sex on the ballot and later in her records, she was elected Superintendent of Schools for Kitsap County in 1881. With her election, Lizzie became one of the first women ever voted into any public office in the Washington Territory.*

An 1881 editorial in the *Seattle Post-Intelligencer* opined, "It may be a good joke to put a woman in nomination, but I do not regard the office of School Superintendent of so little importance as to vote for a woman at the polls. . . ." The majority of Kitsap County's citizens thought otherwise, electing Miss Ordway by 244 votes compared to her male counterpart's 165 votes.

The Office of Superintendent of Kitsap County's Schools had officially existed since 1857; however, no one had ever performed their duties as diligently as Miss Lizzie Ordway. She became the first such official to comply with territorial laws regarding record keeping. In fact, L. M. Ordway was the only superintendent who had ever filed a report with the territorial government as required by law! Her records were meticulously written and organized. In one such report, discussing a teaching contract she noted, "the general rate of pay is $20 - $35 a month for three to six months, and does not include board, but the teacher may dig clams on the Director's beach." The Ordway records are still on file at the Kitsap County Courthouse in Port Orchard.

After eight consecutive years as Kitsap County's school superintendent, Miss Ordway stepped down from the job in 1889, at age sixty-one. She remained on the Kitsap County Board of Education which examined and certified teachers for the district. Miss Lizzie continued to implement ideas ahead of their time. In 1890, she

---

*Antoinette Baker Huntington of Castle Rock was elected Superintendent of Schools for Cowlitz County in 1878 and re-elected in 1880, serving two, two-year terms. Antoinette was in the first group of Mercer Girls to arrive in Seattle with Lizzie Ordway. Clara McCarty Wilt, who also had the distinction of being the very first graduate of the University of Washington in 1876, and for whom McCarty Hall is named, was elected to the position of Superintendent of Schools for Pierce County in 1880.

conducted the first County Teacher's Institute. This "in-service" lasted one week and was attended by twenty teachers who traveled to Port Madison to sharpen their skills. When Lizzie resigned from the board of education she was awarded their highest honor, a "First Grade Certification," by her fellow board members for her years of service to the district. Lizzie had witnessed the Kitsap County School District's growth from two districts, in its infancy, to twenty—fourteen of which were created by her.

In 1891, Lizzie retired to Seattle where she lived with sea Captain Sylvanus Libby and his wife, Sarah. At age sixty-five, in 1893, Lizzie became the assistant to University of Washington Professor Edmond S. Meany in preparing Washington State's education exhibit for the Chicago World's Fair. Her part of the exhibit was to illustrate the quality and availability of good education in the infant state. Easterners were reportedly extremely surprised and pleased to find the high caliber of education in the Pacific Northwest.

Lizzie Ordway died suddenly of cancer on September 22, 1897, at the age of sixty-nine. The Libby family had her buried in their family plot in Lake View Cemetery, where Seattle's pioneers are interred. In 1989, the Bainbridge Island Historical Society nominated Lizzie Ordway to the Washington State Historical Society's Hall of Fame in recognition of her contributions to the Northwest. ⚜

Isabel Friedlander Arcasa

1889–1992

Custodian of Colville Heritage

*H*unting deep in the forests of the Cascade Mountains, the band of natives froze in their tracks and stared in amazement. There in the clearing, standing just where they had last seen him exactly one year ago, was their fellow Wenatchee tribesman. He stood with his arms folded over his chest, staring straight ahead as if in a trance. A strange dog was by his side. The dog barked once at the approaching hunters, then sat silently next to his master.

Eventually, they were able to rouse the man from his trance-like state. He told of being captured and held prisoner by a band of Sasquatches—the mammoth, hair-covered creature, also known as Bigfoot. For one year he had lived in their cedar bark shelters and shared their food as an equal. The Sasquatches were great hunters who were able to scamper up steep inclines and shoulder heavy loads of game. They hunted by night, leaving their crude bark houses and returning early in the morning with game. The Indian learned the signals with which the band communicated. Their sounds were much like the hooting of owls. After he lived with them for one year, the Sasquatches brought the man back to the exact spot where they found him. They hypnotized him and left a dog with him for protection.

FATHER TOM CONNOLLY, S.J., SACRED HEART MISSION, DE SMET, IDAHO

Isabel Friedlander Arcasa and her mother "Elizabeth."

That Wenatchee tribesman was Isabel Friedlander Arcasa's great-great-great grandfather. "The reports of the big foot prints are nothing new. We Indian people know all about those dark people even if we have never seen them." This story has been passed down through Isabel's family for generations, and is regarded not as legend, but as family heritage.

Isabel Friedlander Arcasa was well known and respected for her great storytelling ability. Through Isabel, tribal lore and traditions going back thousands of years were kept and passed on to today's generations. For all of her 102 years, Isabel remained sharp witted and maintained a wonderful sense of humor. She loved to share her tales with everyone around her.

In the Indian way, Isabel had many names throughout her long life. The first girl born after five boys, her mother called her "Kee-arna," meaning "little girl." When her brother Bill could not pronounce the word, the family shortened her name to "Wana." As she grew older her mother gave her the name of her Skokomish great-grandmother, "Ti-men-wy."

Then while visiting her grandmother, she met an old woman of the San Poil Tribe to whom her grandmother had given shelter. One day the feeble old woman called young Isabel to her bedside and whispered to her, "I do not have long to live. When I die, I want you to carry on my name, 'K-new-teet-kw.' I want you to have my things and keep my name alive." The old woman then handed Isabel a long string of copper, Hudson's Bay beads, a necklace of blue and white glass beads, and two ceremonial pipes. Finally, most Indians at this time had English names as well as Indian names. She was baptized "Isabel" by a Catholic priest.

The Wenatchee, Chelan, and Entiat tribes accepted Catholicism around 1870 when Father Urban Grassi founded his mission in the area. Isabel's grandfather, Chief Tsil-hoo-sas-ket of the "Entee-etkw," or Entiat Tribe, was baptized Catholic but balked when Father Grassi told him he must give up one of his two wives. Chief Tsil-hoo-sas-ket was married to Isabel's grandmother Sts-kul-nas-ket, as well as to her younger sister, La-mee-iy. Being a good Catholic, Sts-kul-nas-ket, christened Suzanne, told her husband that she would leave him so that he could marry La-mee-iy, or Rosalie, in the Catholic Church. Suzanne's children were grown, but Rosalie still had a small baby. Suzanne left her husband and returned to the camp of her father. Rosalie and Chief Tsil-hoo-sas-ket were then married in the church. Not satisfied with this arrangement, the chief rode into Suzanne's camp one day and asked her to return with him. She refused, but he would not leave. That night, saying she was going to the river to take a bath, Suzanne left camp. She escaped by paddling her canoe and swimming her horse across the Columbia River. Suzanne hid from Tsil-hoo-sas-ket until, after several days waiting, he gave up and returned to his village of Entiat. Chief Tsil-hoo-sas-ket and his brother, Wapato John, became staunch Catholics, building churches for their people in Entiat and Manson, near Lake Chelan.

*   *   *

Isabel Friedlander was born on the banks of the Columbia River on November 22, 1889, the year Washington became a state. She was the daughter of an Entiat Indian mother and white Jewish father. Though the mixing of white men and Indian women was not uncommon in the American West, the story Isabel tells of how she became a Friedlander is truly unique and fascinating.

Isabel's mother was Skn-wheulks, later christened Elizabeth. Elizabeth's father was Tsil-hoo-sas-ket, chief of the Entiat Tribe. His father and grandfather, also named Tsil-hoo-sas-ket, had all been chiefs of the Entiat Tribe. His mother was a member of the Skokomish Tribe from western Washington. Elizabaeth's mother, Sts-kul-nas-ket, or Suzanne, was descended from the Wenatchee and San Poil Tribes.*

When Elizabeth grew older, Chief Tsil-hoo-sas-ket made arrangements with the Moses Band of the Columbia Tribe for his daughter to be married to Chief Moses's younger brother, Tser-men-tsoot. In those days, the Indians arranged trades to find brides for their young men. The Moses people gave Elizabeth's father horses and possessions for his daughter.

Tser-men-tsoot was already married to a woman by the name of In-ha-noomt, who later left her husband. Elizabeth had three children by Tser-men-tsoot; only one, a baby named Mary, lived. One fall, when Mary was two years old, all of the Moses Band camped near Vantage, on the Columbia River, for their horse races. During the races, Elizabeth's husband, Tser-men-tsoot, was killed. It was the custom of these tribes that when a woman was widowed,

---

* In 1872, the U.S. Government established the Colville Reservation, eventually combining eleven separate tribes: the Colville, Arrow Lakes, Columbia, Chelan, Entiat, Wenatchee, Okanogan, San Poil, Methow, Nespelem, and Joseph Band of Nez Perce.

the deceased husband's brother would become her husband. It was then the brother's obligation to provide for and watch out for the widow and her children.

All of the band went into mourning, and they buried Tser-men-tsoot. Chief Moses, Tser-men-tsoot's older brother, attended the funeral, but after it was over, he told his people it was time to move on. Chief Moses took all of Tser-men-tsoot's many racehorses and valuable belongings away with him. He even took with him a small pony belonging to the baby, Mary. In his wake, Elizabeth was left stranded with her baby and a few in-laws. Without possessions, Elizabeth stayed at the Vantage camp throughout the harsh winter.

In the spring, an old woman asked Elizabeth if she wanted to return to her people. The desperate Elizabeth eagerly accepted the invitation. The elder woman gave the young widow a riding horse and a pack horse so she could return with baby Mary to her father's camp.

Elizabeth wasted no time traveling to her family's village in Entiat. Later that fall, Elizabeth went with her aunt and Uncle Louie to a little trading post across from the mouth of Lake Chelan. A soldier from Camp Chelan was running the trading post. His name was Herman Friedlander, but the Indian people called him "Peranik."

Elizabeth was a handsome woman, and Herman Friedlander could not take his eyes off her. Peranik questioned Uncle Louie about Elizabeth. "Gee, that's sure a beautiful woman! I sure would like to have her for my wife." Uncle Louie replied, "Oh, you can't have anything to do with her; she is just a widow." The soldier was undaunted, "Well, you tell her if she ever wants to get married, that I'd sure like to marry her!" Uncle Louie told Elizabeth of the conversation during the trip home.

While Elizabeth and her aunt and uncle were in Chelan, Chief Moses arrived at the camp of Elizabeth's father, Chief Tsil-hoo-sas-ket. Moses exclaimed, "I am going to come and get my little niece and my brother's wife to marry now. I will bring you some horses, saddles, blankets and valuables." Tsil-hoo-sas-ket agreed, following the Indian custom that a man could marry his deceased brother's wife and eager to obtain horses, saddles, and blankets from the other chief.

Upon returning from the trip to the trading post in Chelan, Elizabeth's father told her of Moses's visit. Elizabeth was furious, when she heard of Moses's intentions. She was angry at the way Chief Moses had left her all alone with no horses in Vantage. Elizabeth declared, "I would never marry Moses, even if he was the last man on earth! Does he not realize what he has done to us? What he did to his little niece, when he took everything away from us and left us stranded? If it had not been for some good people, we would have been lost."

Elizabeth told her Uncle Louie, "You just take me back to the Chelan Trading Post tomorrow. I will marry that white man!"

The next day Elizabeth and her Uncle Louie traveled to the trading post in Chelan. Elizabeth spoke no English, so her Uncle Louie explained to Herman Friedlander the situation with Chief Moses. "She says she doesn't want him. She says she'll marry you." Herman Friedlander found the nearest justice of the peace and they were married that day!

A few weeks later, Chief Moses rode into Entiat with his string of horses for Chief Tsil-hoo-sas-ket. Elizabeth's father had to decline the horses, telling Moses, "I'm sorry, but your sister-in-law went to Chelan and got married to that white man, Peranik." With that, Moses became enraged. "I am going over there, and I'm going to kill him for taking my wife." So he left his string of horses right there and rode to the trading post.

In Chelan, Elizabeth and Herman were living in a square, canvas soldier's tent. The couple heard a rider approaching at a frantic pace. Herman took his gun outside to greet the rider. As he rode up,

Moses hollered, "You took my wife! I am going to kill you! She is my wife!"

"No!" exclaimed Herman, "She is my wife. We were married by a justice of the peace."

Moses insisted, "She was my brother's wife, so now she is my wife. I am going to kill you!"

"Well, go ahead and shoot," said Herman as he leveled his rifle directly at the chief.

When Moses saw the rifle pointing at him, he became silent. He turned his horse around and rode off, never to return.

For the first few years of their marriage, Herman and Elizabeth lived in Chelan where he ran a small store and saloon. Herman Friedlander had been born into a wealthy East Coast family, but his father disowned him for marrying a full-blooded Indian woman. Herman's two brothers, Frank and Sam, also came west and founded jewelry stores bearing their name in Seattle and Portland.

From Chelan, Elizabeth, Herman, and Mary moved up the Columbia River to Lincoln, across from the San Poil Tribes's Village of White Stone, where Elizabeth's family lived. Herman bought a farm with an orchard and ran a store in the nearby town of Wilbur. The Friedlanders lived happily and had seven children together: Louie, Sam, Herman, Bill, Isabel, Millie, and Ed. Elizabeth and Herman never spoke the same language, though they probably both spoke some Chinook jargon. The children spoke the languages of both their parents and they grew up paddling canoes back and forth across the river between their farm and the San Poil village of cabins and tepees, where their grandparents lived.

Herman Friedlander died of a heart ailment when Isabel was only eight years old. Elizabeth eventually sold the farm and store and moved to the White Stone Village with her parents. In those days, many generations lived under one roof so houses were full with beds covering every inch of the floor at night. Elizabeth later married an Indian man, Charlie Comedale, who died within a year of their marriage.

At the age of six, Isabel and her brothers were sent to the Indian boarding school in Tonasket. When the school burned, Isabel was transferred to the mission schools in Omak and Ward. At just seven years of age, Isabel took her five-year-old sister, Millie, and ran away from school. Her older brother found the sisters and returned them to the school.

The nuns at the mission schools punished the students when they spoke their native Indian languages. After three years of such treatment, the children could barely understand their aunt when she came to take them home. Once home, they regained fluency in their language quickly. Isabel was then sent to school at Fort Spokane where she remained until she was fifteen.

Arranged marriages were still common among Indian people when Isabel was a young girl. Trading horses and cattle with Isabel's stepfather, a man arranged a marriage between fourteen-year-old Isabel and his son. In spite of her mother and aunt's objections and Isabel's cries, the two youngsters were married by a priest. Upon leaving the church, other children teased Isabel and in anger, she threw her wedding ring into the dirt and ran off. The two never lived together as husband and wife.

When she was eighteen, a man from the Umatilla Tribe named Julius LaCourse asked for her hand. Worried about the validity of her first marriage, Isabel consulted a priest who told her he would have to write a letter to the Pope. A month later, the papal letter arrived and dictated, "This woman is not an animal that can be sold. Her parents cannot accept presents and sell her like an animal. Her first marriage is annulled."

Isabel married Julius LaCourse and they moved to Pendleton, Oregon. Five children were born to them: Herman, Melvin, Maybelle, and two babies that died in infancy. The family moved where there was work—living in Pendleton, Nespelem, Quincy, Taholah, and Seattle. All of the family worked as migrants, following the crops during the summer, then settling in so the children could attend school in the fall. When her daughter, Maybelle, became sick with tuberculosis, Isabel took a job at Cushman Hospital in Tacoma to be near her.

Julius was a talented musician. He played violin, with Isabel who played piano, in a dance band that played for grange hall dances on weekends. With their children lying beside them on a mattress they brought from home, Isabel and Julius played late into the night.

After twenty-three years of marriage, Isabel gave Julius an ultimatum—he had to quit drinking or she would leave him. When he refused to give up the bottle, she left, divorcing him, although she remained a practicing Catholic. She met her next husband, Marcel Arcasa, while she was working at a youth camp on the Colville Reservation.

Isabel knew a lifetime of hard labor, working as both a cook and waitress. She plowed fields, worked farms, nursed the sick, and acted as a midwife. As a midwife she brought twenty-eight babies into the world and saved the lives of two of their mothers.

Besides raising her own three children, she raised five orphans. In her eighties, she took in her three-year-old great-grandson when his parents were killed.

For her tireless work on behalf of the church and community, Isabel received a papal blessing and Pro Ecclesia Et Pontifice award from the Catholic Church. Always looking after those in need, she canned fruits and vegetables to give hungry families to tide them over through the winters. Young priests were taken under her wing as soon as they moved to her town of Nespelem.

In 1989, Isabel celebrated her 100th birthday, the same year the state of Washington celebrated its centennial. The Eastern Washington Historical Society awarded her the honor of "Pioneer of the

Year." Along with other centenarians, Isabel was invited to an honorary dinner at the State Capitol. Seated next to Governor Booth Gardner, she entertained him with stories of capturing and racing wild horses in her youth. She was not afraid of the wild ones she explained, it was the tame horses that always bucked her off!

Though most of her prized possessions (including woven baskets, beaded bags, moccasins, dresses, and two tepees) burned in a house fire, Isabel was rich in family and friends. She had grandchildren, great-grandchildren, and even great-great-grandchildren at the time of her death, not to mention her countless nieces and nephews. Many accomplished women can be counted among Isabel's descendants, including her niece Lucy Friedlander Covington, who was a Colville tribal councilwoman of great renown. A tireless champion of Indian rights, it has been said that without Lucy's efforts, the Colville Reservation might have been lost to the Termination Bills of the 1960s. Isabel's granddaughter, Anita Dupris, is an attorney, who has worked for years as a judge in the Colville tribal court system.

Isabel passed away on April 24, 1992, at the age of 102. As a legacy to her people, Isabel left behind many stories and legends in the form of manuscripts and tapes of interviews she gave in her twilight years. Always happy to be interviewed, she told her friend, Father Tom Connolly, as he prepared audiotapes of her histories, "I don't care if anyone hears my voice after I'm gone. That's the only way I can haunt you folks!" ⚜

KATHLEEN ROCKWELL

1876–1957

Klondike Kate

*H*idden on the banks of the roaring river, the young woman dressed in boys' clothing crouched, silently waiting for just the right moment. As the men aboard the vessel released the mooring lines and began to shove off, the lithe figure jumped from shore. She missed the boat deck and splashed into the icy, churning waters. Somehow she managed to get a hand on the boat and clung on desperately as her body surfed the rapids. Coming to her rescue, the burly oarsmen pulled her aboard with little effort.

The ruckus caught the attention of a nearby Mountie on shore who shouted out, "Stop in the name of the Queen!" The Canadian Mountie continued to bellow orders, fuss, and fume as the scow headed toward the rapids, but there was little he could do. Drenched, but victorious, Kathleen waved at him triumphantly, as the square boat proceeded toward the seething froth of the Whitehorse and Five Finger Rapids.

"My trip through Miles Canyon and Whitehorse Rapids was perhaps the most exciting trip I ever made. That man at the giant oar-rudder muscled us through with great, uncanny skill," Kate reminisced.

Kathleen Rockwell

So began the gold rush adventures of Kathleen Rockwell, "Queen of the Yukon," the dance hall girl from Spokane, Washington, later dubbed "Klondike Kate." From the moment the long-legged beauty with the reddish gold locks walked down the gangplank into Dawson City, she captivated the hearts of the crusty Klondike miners. The large, barnlike dance hall and theater had featured many a pretty girl, but it was Kate who electrified the stage at the Savoy. Her flame dance was a show stopper, during which she twirled yards of bright red chiffon around her limber form and through the air, electrifying the stage.

Kate was in her twenties when she made it aboard the ship that was headed north to seek riches, and she quickly became a legend—the darling of the North. Queen of the Klondike, Belle of Dawson, Yukon Queen, Sweetheart of the Sourdoughs—Klondike Kate was wined and dined by rough, tough, free spending prospectors who threw buckskin pouches of gold dust (called pokes) at her feet when she danced.

As a young girl, raised in Spokane, Washington, Kate predicted, "I'm going to see the whole world when I grow up!"

*　*　*

Kathleen Eloisa Rockwell was born in Junction City, Kansas, on October 4, 1876, to Martha Alice (Murphy) Rockwell and John W. Rockwell. As she aged, the year of Kate's birth got later and later, and she commonly cited her birth year as 1880. When Kate was a small child, her parents separated (Kate claimed to have no recollection of her father) and Mrs. Rockwell married her divorce attorney, Frank A. Bettis. Bettis moved his new family, including Kathleen, to Spokane where he was appointed Circuit Court Judge for the State of Washington in Spokane County.

Judge Bettis became a wealthy, political official, well known throughout the Inland Northwest. The Bettis family home was among the largest and grandest manors in the city. Kathleen had a governess, while her mother had a maid and a cook. Kate remembers the cook telling her, "Some day you'll grow up to be a very fine lady like your mother and have a great fine house like this for your own. That is, if you learn to mind your manners, Kathleen."

Judge Bettis adored young Kathleen, known to her family as Kitty, and provided her with every luxury. No one in Spokane would have imagined that this pampered, indulged girl, being groomed to take her place in Spokane's "high society," was destined to become a Yukon dance hall queen!

A gypsy at heart, Kathleen was impulsive and daring. Riding her father's well-bred, trotting horses, she would race them into a frothy lather. Playing hooky from school was a favorite pastime; she bought picnic food on her father's accounts and would treat her friends to outdoor feasts. When her mother caught on and canceled her credit with the merchants, Kate simply changed vendors. Always the showman, Kitty draped lace curtains around herself and danced on the lawn of the great house, performing for her neighbors.

Her good heart also showed at an early age. When their Spokane neighborhood nearly burned to the ground, eight-year-old Kathleen invited her neighbors whose homes had been burned to stay at the Bettis Manor. More than one hundred guests took her up on her offer, filling the house with cots for two weeks.

Since Spokane's upper echelon sent their children to boarding school, Mrs. Bettis decided that would be in Kate's best interest. Kathleen was sent to St. Paul's Academy for Girls in Minnesota. In school, Kathleen enjoyed music, but not mathematics which she would bribe classmates to do for her. Under strict supervision of the nuns, the lively Kathleen often found herself in trouble. Once during study hall, Kathleen, ever the performer, danced the Highland Fling to the delight of her classmates and dismay of the Sisters. The nuns punished her by locking her in the bathroom for the rest of the day. Remembering it was bath day for the nuns, Kate ran the hot water out, so the sisters would have to bathe in cold water. The mischievous girl then removed dirty towels from a hamper and stuffed them down the drain.

When Judge Bettis and Kathleen's mother separated, her heartbroken mother decided to move to New York, where she was unknown, to forget her sorrow. Kathleen and her mother set sail from Seattle on a freighter. Passengers were not allowed on the ship, so the Rockwell women were deemed "stewardesses." Before the Panama Canal was dug, ships sailed around the horn of South America. Mrs. Bettis planned to leave Kathleen with her half-brother who lived in Valparaiso, Chile, while she found a place to live in New York City.

On the exotic cruise, Kathleen saw whales, porpoises, and tropical birds from the ship's deck. When sailors caught the beautiful birds using baited hooks, the tender-hearted Kathleen freed them. Not all was serene though—Kathleen once found herself amidst a drunken sailor's brawl in Valparaiso.

During the trip, Kathleen became engaged to the ship's first officer. Alarmed, her mother placed her in the Sacred Heart Convent when they reached Valparaiso. As a rare "gringa" in Latin America, Kathleen was quite an attraction. Not knowing Spanish, she answered "Si" to all questions and soon found herself with a bevy of suitors. Encouraged, these young Latin lovers threw notes to Kate over the convent's walls. She became particularly enamored with a Spanish attaché and accepted a proposal from the handsome Latino. When her mother heard of the engagement, she quickly sent for Kathleen to join her in New York.

Mrs. Bettis had no concept of money. She had taken the proceeds from the sale of their Spokane house and continued to live in her accustomed manner of luxury until her money ran out. The Rockwell women found themselves penniless and alone in New York City, with eighty-three dollars between them. Mrs. Bettis went to work in a factory making shirtwaists, while sixteen-year-old Kate began to look for work. Each evening she read the classified ads aloud to her mother in their tiny apartment. One day an ad caught her eye, "Chorus Girls wanted—no experience necessary." Knowing her proper mother would never approve, Kate secretly answered the ad.

Always fond of dancing, she auditioned and was hired by the production company. Her mother was horrified when she heard of her daughter's new found occupation. Once Mrs. Bettis had calmed down, she accepted Kate's decision but never knowingly let her perform unchaperoned.

When the show opened in Pittsburgh, Kate went with the company without telling her mother. The show flopped, and the company went broke. Stranded, Kate and another girl went to a church and prayed for a way home. Then, the two young dancers stole into a railroad yard and jumped a box car to New York. With their last pennies, they purchased stale doughnuts for the ride. In New York, they walked 183 blocks to the room of a friend to clean up before going home. Mrs. Bettis had alerted the police about her missing daughter and was beside herself with worry when Kate finally turned up. She forbade her daughter from the stage, but the chorus girl life was now in Kate's blood. Again defying her mother, Kitty took her next job in Coney Island. Her mother reluctantly agreed but set a curfew. Kate barely had time to dress after her last act and ride the street car home by her mother's deadline.

It was a letter from a childhood friend from Spokane that lured Kate Rockwell west again. The friend wrote of high-paying jobs in "continuous vaudeville." There was a job opening, so Kathleen headed west.

Her first night on the job, Kate signed in at the variety theater. Following her stage performance, she returned to her dressing room to wait for her next show. Suddenly her bell rang and she was told to sit in one of the curtained booths or "boxes." An old school friend joined her asking if she would let him buy her a bottle of wine. "Oh, no thank you," the naive Kate replied, "I do not drink wine." The waiter nearly fainted! Crying, she ran to her dressing room where one of the performers explained the role to Kate. Not only were the girls to sing and dance, but between acts they were to flirt with the customers—enticing them into buying expensive bottles of wine. As hostesses, they earned a commission for every bottle they sold. The dancer showed Kate how to pour her glass of wine into the spittoons when the customers were not looking.

She was next booked into the People's Theater in Seattle and a few weeks later, the Savoy in Victoria, British Columbia. Kate became the theater company's starlet, presenting two new flashy songs each week. The owners of the Savoy Theater guarded the virtue of the girls in the company. The performers had a curfew, and every night they were checked into their rooms over the theater. Still, Mrs. Bettis was appalled when she heard of her daughter's employment in variety theaters. Kate appeased her by saying she would send for her mother when she had saved enough money.

Yet it was hard for Kate to save money when she was continuously helping others. When she finally had enough to bring her mother west, she found a girl in her company in need of hospitalization. Generously, Kathleen donated her savings and took up a collection for the sick dancer. A local newspaper reporter heard the story and wrote about Kate's efforts. This was the first of many stories to be written about Kate. Still, her mother was not pleased.

Kate's second write-up was a review of her performance at Seattle's Comique Theater. A reporter wrote that she sang and danced with a "French Flair." Her picture was printed in newspapers and magazines, and she became one of the first pinup girls in the North-west.

The headline for the Seattle paper the morning of July 17, 1897, changed Kate's life again. The bold type read, "A Ton of Solid Gold—A Rush to the Clondyke [sic]—A Rush to the North—All Daft Over Gold." The ship Portland had docked in Seattle, bringing gold toting miners and the beginning of a hysteria which became known as the Klondike Gold Rush. Before long, the towns of Skagway, Dyea, and Dawson City became household words. Every-one knew the path to riches ran over the treacherous White and Chilkoot Passes.

Kate began moving north, taking a job in Bennett, British Co-lumbia, a gold-crazy town where would-be-miners bought their out-fits and built scows, or flat riverboats, to take them upriver to the Yukon in search of the precious metal. Kate caught gold fever and longed to go north. The Canadian Mounted Police, or "Mounties," were stopping women from traveling the river to Whitehorse and into Dawson City. Kate concealed her sex beneath boys' clothing and leapt aboard a rickety old scow to travel through the raging Whitehorse Rapids.

A letter was waiting at Whitehorse, inviting Kate to return to Victoria, British Columbia, for a job as a dancer in a large burlesque, musical comedy company that was forming to play in Dawson. Kate returned to British Columbia, auditioned, got the job, and again headed north to Dawson, with the Savoy Theatrical Company. The 173 member company was the largest ever to play the Klondike. The show opened in 1900, featuring dancing girls, as well as a full orchestra.

Kate was initially disappointed to find that the streets of Dawson were not paved with gold and the theater she was to star in was nothing but a big, empty, barnlike structure. Before one week had passed, the Savoy had become the entertainment center of

YUKON ARCHIVES, NATIONAL MUSEUM OF CANADA

Kathleen Rockwell

Dawson and all of the Yukon Territory, and Kate was happy to be a part of it all. The cavernous building came alive with the whir of the roulette wheel, clinking of glasses, shuffling of cards, and band music under the glow of coal oil lamps illuminating the room. The girls were always dressed in the finest modern fashions, but the men were wild and wooly—fresh from the gold fields.

As star of the show, Kate was provided a room above the theater. The elegant room, complete with red and gold wallpaper, oak furniture, lace curtains, and a plush red carpet, even provided a view of the river.

Women were scarce on the streets of Dawson and when they appeared on the sidewalks, they attracted the miner's appreciative stares and whistles. There were three types of women in town: the family women who were married to the miners; entertainers, actresses, and dance hall girls like Kate; and the girls across the river who engaged in the world's oldest profession.

Her first year in Dawson was the happiest of young Kate's life. A strange mixture of people came to the Savoy to have fun; the gold-rich millionaires, gamblers, and dance hall girls all mingled to create a festive atmosphere. The show began at 8:30 P.M., and the girls often did not retire until ten in the morning. They knew all the modern dances, and the miners paid handsomely to dance and drink with the girls. The dancers kept half of the dance money and a quarter of the money spent on each drink. The commission on a bottle of champagne was $7.50. On her best night, Kate earned $750, mostly just for rolling cigarettes and talking with lonely prospectors. Dances were a dollar each, and the music stopped frequently. Waiters sold fifteen-dollar bottles of wine and removed them from the tables when they were still half full. The prospectors had pockets lined with pouches of gold and spent freely, often when they wanted to put aside their loneliness for an evening.

Throughout the frozen winters, the miners lived in isolated, drafty cabins. When the spring thaw came and town was more accessible, they headed for the Savoy looking for company, entertainment, and excitement. When dances pleased the prospectors, they tossed their pokes of gold onto the stage at the dancers' feet. Many came into the Savoy rich and left poor, some men losing as much as $100,000 gambling and free-spending in one night.

Offstage, the girls wore gold nugget jewelry and designer dresses over silk petticoats that rustled when they walked. Kate ordered gowns from Paris, one costing as much as fifteen hundred dollars. Her lingerie was handmade in France. The stage gowns sparkled with rhinestones, seed pearls, spangles, and sequins. Kate always wore tights on stage. Her most daring outfit involved a black satin coat, which she removed to reveal a short, rhinestone-studded costume with pink tights. Risqué in its day, this costume would be considered mild now. Had any of the girls shown a bare leg, the show would have been shut down.

Kate loved the excitement as well as the great outdoors. She kept horses and dogs and mushed dog sleds throughout the icy winters. Even while living the high life of a dance hall queen, Kate cared for others. She housed a pregnant girl with tuberculosis in a cabin near the dance hall. The girl was poor, sick, and had been abandoned by the baby's father. After a performance one evening, Kate slipped out to check on the girl and found her giving birth. The young mother died in childbirth, so Kate took the baby boy under her care. She kept him until he was three years old, at which time she found him foster parents in "the States." Always remaining anonymous, she sent money for the child's college education and followed his career. The man became a successful engineer, but Kathleen refused to ever disclose his identity. Even though he never knew of Klondike Kate's influence on his life, she thought of him as her son. This was the only child Kathleen Rockwell ever "had."

Full of the holiday spirit one Christmas season, the miners crowned Kate "Queen of the Yukon." Cutting her a crown from a tin can and impaling candles on the jagged points, they lit them for her grand coronation. Kate danced in the glow of her lighted crown, adorned in her expensive Paris gown. The men loved the dance, cheering wildly. Her long braids were soon coated with wax which would not wash out. She became the first in town to have "bobbed" hair.

That night, standing in the crowded room watching the luminescent, dancing Klondike Kate, was a quiet Norwegian miner. During the excitement Kate never noticed the silent man. When the chaos subsided, she spotted the blonde Scandinavian watching her.

Drawn to him, she approached, took his hand, and asked him to dance. This was the first man she had ever had to ask to dance. Shyly, he answered in his thick Norwegian accent that he had just come to watch. "Yoo are yust beautiful." Finding him sweet, Kate talked for awhile, and he told her he would "vait for her."

It was a slick, handsome, smooth-talking, Greek immigrant though who stole her heart. A natural promoter, Alexander Pantages was a charmer burning with ideas and goals. Most men of the Yukon dressed roughly and usually wore scraggly beards. In sharp contrast, Alex took pains to dress well and was always clean shaven. He was a smooth talker who could also be indifferent or insolent if it didn't suit his needs to be gracious.

When Alex was unemployed, Kate opened her purse strings. She not only supported him, she gave him money so that he could smoke fine cigars, wear imported silk shirts, and dine in elegant restaurants. Kate paid for their room and board as well.

With gold dust gathered from miner's pokes while "giving change," Pantages started his own dance hall, charging miners $12.50 a seat. At its peak, he claimed his theater made eight thousand dollars per day.

In 1901, Alex convinced Kate to leave the Yukon Territory. She purchased a theater in Victoria, British Columbia, but even though it was making money, Pantages told her to sell it. With the money from the sale of her successful theater, Alex bought a theater in Seattle, the Crystal. When the Crystal began to turn a profit, Pantages built theaters in Tacoma, Spokane, Portland, and Vancouver. He became a millionaire from his chain of combination movie/vaudeville theaters.

All the while, Kathleen Rockwell thought herself an equal partner in these ventures. According to her court testimony, Pantages told Kate he needed more money and asked her to travel to Texas where he believed a dance hall girl could still find fortune. In 1903,

Kate went to Texas at his insistence. She sent her earnings home to Alex, and he invested them in his emerging theater dynasty. After a year of performing in Texas, Kate returned to Seattle. There she found her "partner" romantically involved with an eighteen-year-old violinist from one of his theaters. Pantages and Lois Mendenhall were married in March of 1905. Four days later Kate learned of the marriage. Despondent, Kathleen sought the company of her mother, who had moved to Seattle and begun operating a successful Seattle real estate firm.

Kate filed suit against Pantages for breach of promise. *The Seattle Times* headline of May 26, 1905, read, "Uses Her Money Then Jilts the Girl." Alexander admitted that he and Kate had lived together but insisted there were no promises of marriage. He also claimed to have little money. A year after her complaint was filed in King County Superior Court asking for twenty-five thousand dollars in damages, Kate settled the case for five thousand dollars. Heartbroken, she returned to Dawson to attempt a recovery.

With the gold rush over, Dawson was not the same and Kate soon was traveling throughout Alaska and the States with the vaudeville circuit, performing some of her acts on roller skates. Kate's mother, a successful Seattle businesswoman by that time, urged her daughter to quit the stage life and return to Seattle. Compromising, Kate bought "Idlours," a well-known hunting lodge on Hood Canal across Puget Sound from Seattle, using it as a private refuge. She retreated there on many occasions, vacationing from her frantic vaudeville tours.

In 1912, a twisted knee finally forced Kate to retire from life on the stage. Depression set in, and Kate suffered a nervous breakdown. Her doctors ordered a year of rest, so Kate bought a horse, saddle, and six-shooter and rode from Seattle to Medford, Oregon. She wandered central Oregon for a year before returning to Seattle, where in 1914, she met a man who owned a homestead in Bend,

Oregon. Her mother traded four acres of Seattle waterfront and some cash for the property. When she went to see what they had purchased, Kate found 320 acres of sagebrush surrounding a tiny, one room shack. In a dress and high heels, she began grubbing sagebrush and piling up rocks. She felt like giving it up many times, but the beauty and desert sunsets always turned her around. For the first time in her life, she was rested and content, and money was not important to Kathleen E. Rockwell.

Kate married Floyd Warner, a handsome young cowboy, in 1915. Her new husband was a jealous man who wanted to fight anyone addressing his bride as "Klondike Kate." Floyd left their homestead to serve in World War I; after the war they drifted apart.

After three unsuccessful years of ranching (she once owned forty-two head of cattle, but they "sort of drifted"), she found herself broke. Kate took a variety of jobs—ran rooming houses, nursed the sick, washed dishes, and ran restaurants. Through all of this, she kept most of her Yukon gold jewelry. As Kate said in a 1956 interview, "I can remember those queer looks on the faces of customers, seeing me up to my elbows in soap suds, with a thousand dollars worth of diamonds in each ear."

She later returned to Seattle to care for her dying mother. Following her mother's death, Kate continued to take odd jobs throughout Oregon and California. She kept her home in Bend but traveled whenever she had the money. At one point when she was broke in California, she called on her former beau, Alexander Pantages, now a millionaire, for a loan. Alex gave her six dollars.

Later, in 1929, when Alex was accused of attacking a young actress, Kate was called to his defense as a character witness. Pantages's trial ended in a conviction, and he was sentenced to prison for up to fifty years. Three years later, during his appeal, the victim accepted three thousand dollars, to drop the matter, and the case was dismissed.

In 1931, a character from Kate's past read an article about her role in the Pantages Trial in a three-year-old newspaper. Johnny Matson, the shy Norwegian who did not dance, wrote to Kathleen, "I have always been in love with you, Katie, all these years. I never had the courage to tell you before. I have heard that life has not been too good to you. I would like to have the right to take care of you as my wife."

When they met again, Kate, at age fifty-three, told Johnny, "I'm old now." To this he replied, "Yoo look yust the same to me as yoo did years ago, the most beautiful woman a man ever saw." They were married on July 14, 1933, and returned to Dawson on their honeymoon.

With her health no longer up to the Klondike's rugged winters, Kate wintered in Bend while Johnny continued to mine his claim on Matson Creek. Every summer she traveled north to be with him. Twice a year Johnny mushed sixty miles on snowshoes to mail letters to his wife. She went from thinking of Johnny as her "funny little yam and yelly man," to the best man on earth. In 1946, when the letters stopped, Kate sent out an expedition to look for her spouse. Eighty-three-year-old Johnny's frozen body was found on a trail seven miles from his lone cabin. After fifty years in the Yukon, that year was to have been his last, for he had finally agreed to Kate to retire from prospecting in the spring.

At seventy-one, Kate married W. L. Van Duren, an accountant whom she had nursed back to health at her convalescent home in Oregon. The couple wed in Vancouver, Washington, on April 1, 1948. They lived quietly for a number of years until her death.

Several movies based on the life of Klondike Kate were made. While Kate acted as a consultant on some, there were others she disdained. Kate was horrified at Mae West's suggestive performance in *Klondike Annie*, saying, "That picture is a disgrace. Why if any of us girls had acted like Mae West acted on the screen, we would have been handed a blue ticket [fired]."

Kathleen E. Rockwell Warner Matson Van Duren died in Sweet Home, Oregon, on February 21, 1957, at the age of eighty, although her obituaries listed her age as seventy-seven. Kate's ashes were scattered across the central Oregon desert. Forever a "sourdough," Klondike Kate throughout her life lived by her often quoted motto, "Mush on and smile!" ⚜

Fay Fuller
1869–1958

First Lady of Mount Rainier

Peppered with a spray of gravel loosened by the climber above, Fay stepped gingerly along the narrow ledge. Each step was a catalyst for a cavalcade of rocks to break loose from above and tumble down the glacial slope. After surmounting one ledge, another—narrower and steeper—would rise to challenge her. Hour after hour, foot by foot, the climb grew more and more treacherous and burdensome as the party approached the great cliff, the most dangerous obstacle of the climb.

Perched carefully on the peaked spines of glacial ridges, the climbers could look down on either side of them and see that one wrong step would plunge them into the icy world below. One of her fellow climbers loosened his pack in an attempt to toss it ahead, across the moat. When he lost his hold, the bundle was sent spiraling downward into a seemingly bottomless black hole. Nothing was said; all among them knew that one wrong step, and they could easily meet the same fate.

The climbers passed the fearsome ridge only to encounter the next obstacle—a face of sheer ice, fifty feet high. Tied together with ropes, the party moved one foot at a time, waiting for each step

Fay Fuller

before them to be carved out by their guide's hatchet. Time became an enemy as the afternoon sun began to melt away the frozen ground beneath their feet, causing sand and gravel to rain down on the person below.

Upon reaching twelve thousand feet above sea level, Fay's breathing became labored. Having conquered the Great Gibraltar Cliff, the party rested before heading upward on great fields of snow and cascades of glacial ice. Fay carefully searched for a toehold while crossing the next bridge of ice. Blue walls of ice, breaking way to reveal caves that seemed without end, surrounded them.

At one crevasse, there seemed to be no bridge to cross; the guide probed at the ice with his spike. All steps were probed and tested for strength, lest they lead into hidden crevasses. Chunks of snow broke away, emanating loud crashing sounds as they fell to bottomless depths. One portion seemed stable, but the guide examined it from underneath to be sure before scrambling across. Holding the rope tossed over by their guide, the others followed hand over hand up the great incline framed by endless fissures.

Above a dazzling white expanse of snow, the black rim of the volcano's crater was now within sight. A biting wind burned at Fay's skin, pushed her from side to side, and tore at her clothing. The air became thinner and increasingly difficult to breath, yet the peak, closer than ever, was within her reach. She toiled upward.

At 4:30 P.M. on August 10, 1890, twenty-year-old Fay Fuller stood on the top of Mount Rainier. The first woman to accomplish this feat, the young school teacher from Yelm had reached an altitude of 14,411 feet.

Fay's climb brought her recognition from far and wide, but not all of it was positive. In an interview with *The Tacoma News Tribune* in 1950, Fay remembered how her fellow Tacomans were shocked at her adventure. "I was very nearly ostracized in Tacoma because of that trip—a lone woman and four men climbing a mountain, and in that immodest costume."

Initially, Fay tried to ignore the negative comments. Speaking only of her feat, she said "I accomplished what I have always dreamed of and feared impossible, and from my experience nothing could be taken."

Shortly after her return, Fay posed for a photographer against a background of faux ice. She modeled the outfit and gear she had worn on the actual climb. The photograph appeared in newspapers and magazines across the country causing both admiration and admonishment. Occasionally, the photograph was used to show the "proper" mountain climbing attire for women in 1890. The caption under one such photo read, "Fay E. Fuller . . . demonstrated the correct mountain climbing costume in 1890." To this Fay replied, "Proper nothing. It was our dressmaker's idea of what I should wear. She designed it. It certainly caused a lot of talk." She further describes her attire in a 1933 letter:

> The costume. . .will amuse present-day climbers. I had it made at the time when bloomers were unknown and it was considered quite immodest. How anyone could have scrambled over the rocks thus attired is now inconceivable. There were no boots or heavy shoes available for women at the time and I bought the strongest shoes that were sold to boys. I believe the stock was made by a blacksmith at Yelm from a curved shovel handle.

* * *

Fay E. Fuller was born in New Jersey on October 10, 1869, to Ann E. (Morrison) Fuller and Edward N. Fuller. With her family, she moved to Tacoma, Washington Territory, in 1882, where her father became editor of a local newspaper. Following her graduation from high school in Tacoma, Fay took a job teaching school at age fifteen. Her first job was at Rosedale on the Kitsap Peninsula's Henderson Bay. Next, she taught school at the Longfellow School in Tacoma and later in Yelm, a small community south of Tacoma.

On one occasion, Miss Fuller's classroom was visited by Philemon Beecher Van Trump, one of the first climbers to reach Mount Rainier's peak. As Mr. Van Trump told of his exploits, Fay listened, enthralled. She and P. B. Van Trump became friends, and it was this friendship that inspired her great accomplishment.

Always an outdoorswoman, Fay loved the Northwest. She spent many hours riding horseback through tall Northwest timbers. Fay preferred to ride astride the horse like a man, rather than the more proper woman's style of riding sidesaddle. When not in the woods, Fay could be found rowing a boat in the rough Tacoma Narrows' current of Puget Sound. Physical activity was an integral part of her life. For the "healthful benefits of exercise," she performed calisthenics and conducted rifle drills with a group called the Women's Guard.

The daughter and sister of newspaper men, Fay gave up teaching to become a reporter. She began by working for her father who was the editor of several Tacoma papers. She later became the first woman reporter for the *Tacoma Ledger*. In a 1943 interview, Fay described her job, "I covered the waterfront, equity court, the markets—oh, anything and everything. I walked miles from one end of town to the other, holding my skirts out of the dust and mud."

Captivated by Van Trump's mountain climbing experiences, Fay's desire to challenge the great mountain grew. In 1887, Fay Fuller made her first assault on Mount Rainier, climbing to the 8,500 foot elevation. Though excited by her accomplishment, Fay felt frustration as well. She was certain she could go further, but she did not dare to hope for the peak.

One August day in 1890, the Van Trump family invited Fay to join them on a camping trip to the mountain. The campers included

Mr. and Mrs. Van Trump and their ten-year-old daughter, Christine. By horseback, the small party left Yelm on Monday morning, August 4, 1890. A pack horse carried their provisions and tents, and their clothing was packed in saddle bags.

Though she doubted Van Trump would care to climb the mountain again, Fay outfitted herself for the possibility. In Fay's account of her climb, "A Trip to the Summit," which was published in her father's weekly paper, *Every Sunday,* on August 23, 1890, Fay stated she was "dressed in a thick, blue flannel bloomer suit, heavy calfskin boys' shoes, a loose blouse waist with innumerable pockets in the lining, and a small straw hat." She also had packed goggles, had an alpenstock made from a shovel handle with a spike driven into one end, and brought wool blankets which she tied over her shoulder during the climb.

The party traveled across prairies and through timberlands, over narrow trails, rough wagon roads, and through thick brush. Fay and the Van Trumps spent the first night sleeping on straw in a barn belonging to So-To-Lick, or "Indian Henry," "a smart old Klickitat" who owned a valuable farm on a mountain meadow. It was So-To-Lick who had guided Van Trump's 1883 expedition up the mountain as far as the snow line.

They were joined that night by two other parties, one from Yelm and the other from Seattle. The paths of these groups had crossed several times during their five-day trek to the mountain. When all parties had reached the proximity of Paradise Camp, Miss Fuller paid a visit to the other camps and learned of a planned ascent by a party consisting of the Reverend E. C. Smith, pastor of the Seattle Unitarian Church; W. O. Amsden, Seattle photographer; R. R. Parrish of Portland; Len Longmire of Yelm; and others who were ultimately held back by illness. Longmire invited members of the Van Trump party to join them climbing. Here was her chance! Fay wanted to go, but was afraid if she failed to make the summit one of the men would have to leave the climb to take her back to camp. When Len volunteered to return with Fay, should it become necessary, she joined the four mountain climbers.

This was to be the first of many climbs for Len Longmire, a member of a pioneer, Pierce County family. For the next twenty years, Len guided tourists up Mount Rainier for a fee of one dollar per hiker.

On Saturday morning, August 9 at 11 A.M., Fay dressed in her heavy flannels, woolen hose, warm mittens, and goggles. She drove long "caulks and brads" into her boys' shoes, rolled up two blankets containing three-days provisions and strapped them to her back. To avoid sunburn, she blackened her face with charcoal. For a quick snack, Fay placed chocolates into the pockets of her blouse. As she tells it, "I put a good supply of chocolate in those pockets. You can imagine what happened when the sun came out hot on my back."

As they set out, the sun beamed down on their backs, causing their packs to feel increasingly heavier and hotter. They ascended long steep snowfields, over ledges of rock, and over one small crevasse that afternoon. The group spent the night at Camp Muir, arising at 4:30 A.M. on August 10, 1890, to venture forth into the most difficult part of the climb. Breakfasting only on raisins and prunes, and with no water as the streams had frozen over during the night, they set out up the southeast slope of the mountain.

Twelve hours later, the four men and one woman stood "on the tip top of Mount Tahoma," as Mount Rainier was then called. Fay describes the pinnacle moment, "It was a heavenly moment; nothing was said—words cannot describe [the] scenery and beauty, how could they speak for the soul!"

Each of the climbers left a remembrance at the summit. They carved their names in the ice, and deposited hair pins, a sardine can, a brandy flask, and tin cup at the top of Mount Rainier. Fay's hair pins were found by the next party up the mountain, the Hitchcock party. They teased Fay that it proved to them that a woman really had made it to the summit.

Descending, the climbers found they could hardly stand due to the ferocious wind. They found shelter in a crater surrounded by steam jets, "looking as if a row of boiling tea kettles had been placed along the ridge." A fine spray from the steam vents drenched their clothing, forcing them to move their camp to an ice cave. Before resting for the night, each climber bathed their feet in whiskey (yet another scandalous event!). Freezing cold and sickened by exhaustion and sulphur fumes from deep within the dormant volcano, Fay suffered nausea and was unable to sleep during the night. She spent the night listening to the distant roar of avalanches cascading down the mountain's slopes. When she rose, her shoes had frozen stiff and had to be melted over a steam vent. She hated to leave the shelter, finding the wind blowing so fiercely she could barely keep her balance.

The descent had to be made rapidly in order to reach the Great Gibraltar Cliff during the morning hours. Retracing the previous day's path over the snowfield, down the crags, slipping on pumice covered glacial faces, the party went without water for six hours and ate very little. Once at the Gibraltar Ledges, they found the steps they had carved in the ice were melted by the afternoon sun and had to be re-cut. The steps, cut at intervals easy for a man to reach, were more difficult for the smaller Miss Fuller to span. Descending over the cliff's rock ledge frightened Fay more than climbing up it had.

Slipping and sliding on their backsides down steep slopes like frolicking children, the group reached camp by afternoon. Fay was a sight! Her lips, nose, and other parts of her face were swollen out of proportion by sun and windburn. She suffered burning eyes and peeling wrists, and she found it hard to walk for several days. Her only regret was that she had left her camera at base camp rather than taking it with her to the summit, though she acknowledged it would have proved burdensome to carry. In spite of an accident involving his camera, Amsden was able to take some beautiful photographs, for which he had numerous orders.

After the climb, Fay Fuller and Len Longmire expressed mutual admiration for one another's accomplishment. She said of him that, "dressed in summer clothing and without gloves he was plucky enough to reach the top, a statement that means something even if one is prepared for it." Longmire stated often that Miss Fuller repeatedly refused assistance from the men, even in the most dangerous spots. She emphasized that if she could not reach the top without male help, she did not deserve to make it at all!

Fay's own account of her historic climb was published within weeks of the event in *Every Sunday*. Enthralled with the experience of climbing, Fay published every account she could find about early climbs of Mount Rainier. The publications of such expeditions, and of her own climb, piqued great interest in the sport of mountain climbing.

Fay's second climb, in 1897, proved nearly as historic as her first. A charter member of a Portland-based, mountain climbing club, the "Mazamas," Fay joined two hundred members of the group in an assault on the mountain. This was the largest group to ever camp on Mount Rainier to date.

On July 27, 1897, fifty-eight of the Mazamas, including several women, reached the summit, where they burned a red fire on the top of Mount Rainier to signal Tacoma of their successful climb.

Fay Fuller and seven other Mazamas chose to spend the night on the summit. The other fifty descended to Camp Muir. Encouraged by the bright night to continue, some of the hikers left Camp Muir, guided by the light of the moon. Edgar McClure, a chemistry professor from the University of Oregon, began his moonlight descent carrying with him his yard-long, mercurial barometer with which he had calculated the altitude of the mountain at 14,528 feet.

McClure slipped and fell to his death without making a sound. His climbing partner believed he had fainted due to cold, fatigue, hunger, and dehydration. McClure's death was the first recorded climbing tragedy on Mount Rainier. Thus, Fay Fuller's second expedition recorded another "first." Two additional climbers nearly met the same fate the next day when they fell into a deep crevasse but survived.

In addition to the *Tacoma Ledger* and her father's papers, Fay wrote for a weekly called *The Stage*, sponsored by a Tacoma theater, and worked for a time in Pendleton, Oregon. In 1900, Fay left Tacoma on an assignment to cover the Chicago World's Fair. When the fair closed, she took a job with the Chicago *Inter-Ocean*, then later took reporting jobs in Washington D.C. and New York. In 1905, she married Fritz Von Briesen, a prominent New York attorney, and gave up her reporting career. Fay had two children, a son and a daughter and lived for many years in New York. Her last visit to Mount Rainier was in 1950, when at the age of eighty she traveled as high as Paradise Lodge, where she was an honored guest on the mountain.

Fay Fuller Von Briesen passed away on May 27, 1958, in Santa Monica, California, at the age of eighty-eight. Fay predicted that her example would be followed by "a good many women." In fact, there were two women climbers to the summit in 1891, Susan Longmire (Len's thirteen-year-old daughter) and Edith Corbet (whose illness had prevented her from climbing with Fay's party). Fay recommended that all who live within view of the much revered Mount Rainier have the opportunity, and "want to begin life anew might profitably spend a few weeks next summer on its hillside, if they want to fall in love with the world again. The beauty and grandeur and inspiration you will find there will add new life." ⚜

OLIVE SPORE RYTHER
1849–1934

Mother Ryther—Mother to Thousands

*T*he small face peeked timidly from behind the humbly dressed man standing in the doorway of the imposing mansion. His sad eyes downcast, hat in his hands, the beaten man had come to ask for help. Would Mother Ryther have room for his son? The boy's mother had died when he was an infant. An elderly grandmother had taken her place, caring for the child while his father worked in a mill on the outskirts of town to support them. Now, the grand-mother had died and there was no one to care for the boy. Kindness and empathy radiated from the frail, bent woman, as she urged them into the home that had been a grand manor in its day. The faded wood-paneled entry and stairway hinted at well-worn elegance.

Still clinging tightly to his father's hand, the boy was taken outside to a swing situated on an endless rolling lawn. There, two little girls dressed in their Sunday finest, with ribbons neatly tied in their hair, were swinging. Scooting to the side, the girls patted the seat of the swing and urged the boy to join them. Tempting as this was, the shy child hung back in his father's shadow, refusing their offer.

This plan failing, the elderly matron led the boy and his father

Mother Ryther poses with a few of her charges.

to the boys' side of the large yard where groups of youngsters were engaged in a variety of noisy, active games. Although the child became engrossed watching the boys at play, he still refused to let go of his father's hand.

The father and son were then invited to supper. Here they were separated—the boy seated at the children's table, the father with the adults. Still, the boy's eyes never left his father. Following dinner, the children filed out into the large yard and the games began anew. Soon, the shy newcomer was running about the lawn in a game of tag, as his father quietly slipped out the door.

In this manner, like so many before him, the young boy became part of Mother Ryther's family at the Ryther Child Home. Olive Ryther dedicated fifty-one of her eighty-five years to creating a home for orphaned and unfortunate women and children. More than three thousand children were cared for by the legendary Mother Ryther.

Mother Ryther never refused a child or a parent in need, no matter what the circumstances. She asked one dollar per week to board children, but if the parents could not pay, the child stayed anyway. One shabbily clothed mother showed up at the home with her small children in tow—all poorly dressed as well. She pleaded with Mother Ryther to take her young, saying she could not pay for their care. Of course, the children were admitted. A few days later, one of Mother Ryther's matrons spied the same mother, now fashionably dressed, drinking in a saloon downtown. The matron hurried home to inform Mother Ryther. Expecting to elicit a response of ire from Mother Ryther, the matron was stunned to find the anger directed at her when Mother replied, "Well, what of it!" banging her fist on the table for emphasis.

Olive Ryther chose the workers at her home for their need of a job rather than their qualifications. In turn, she received dedicated service from loyal employees. The cook at the home was a grossly overweight woman who had previously worked as the fat lady in the circus. The cook's work could be, at times, sub par, and she was not always gentle with the children, but Mother Ryther overlooked her faults for years because the woman needed the work.

* * *

Olive Hannah Spore was born in Iowa on March 15, 1849, the child of Scottish immigrants. On May 7, 1867, at the age of eighteen, Olive married a young carpenter, Noble Ryther. The couple had three daughters: Amy, Ella, and Mae Bird. Olive ("Ollie") and Noble were dedicated members of the Methodist Church, continually looking for ways to serve the ministry. Inspired to enter missionary service, Noble Ryther, a Civil War veteran, left his family and moved west to the Washington Territory in 1874.

In Seattle, he lived at the City Mission on the waterfront overlooking Elliott Bay. At the same time, he staked a claim on the east side of Lake Washington, north of present-day Kirkland. He divided his time between developing his claim east of the lake and traveling by canoe across Lake Washington to the mission. Building his home proved difficult as he related, "There was plenty of wood out there, but all of it wet."

As a missionary in early Seattle, Noble supplied spiritual guidance, food, clothing, shelter, and sometimes money for indigent men. He also worked clearing land and building homes for others to earn money which, for nine long years, he sent home to his wife and three daughters in Iowa. Seattle was a rough logging town full of saloons and houses of ill repute. Noble did not want to raise his family in this wild city.

After nine years in Seattle, Noble was able to finish building a cabin on a lot in Seattle and he was ready to send for his family. Olive and her three daughters rode the sooty, grimy locomotive west to Seattle in the summer of 1883.

Mrs. Ryther immediately joined her husband, Noble, working at the City Mission on Commercial Street (now First Avenue). The mission lodged homeless and destitute men at a charge of five cents a meal, if they could afford it. Olive took over the cooking at the mission where the Rythers and their daughters took their meals with the homeless men.

Within a year of arriving in Seattle, Olive gave birth to the couple's son, Allen. Soon after, she also became mother to four orphaned children. In a dark, dreary cabin on a typical Seattle blustery, wet, winter day, Olive found herself nursing a dying mother. The Long family lived in dire poverty; the woman's absentee husband had last been seen in a waterfront bar. As she lay dying, the feeble mother turned to Olive and pleaded, "What will become of my poor children?" Olive assured the destitute mother that she would take in the children as her own. After their mother's death, the four Long children moved into the simple log home of Olive and Noble Ryther to be raised with their own four children. With their home now bursting at the seams, the Rythers moved to a house at 813 Alder Street, near what is now Harborview Hospital.

While working at the mission, Olive became concerned for the "fallen women," or prostitutes, she saw daily on the streets of Seattle. She began visiting with them, assisting with their problems, and attempting to rescue them from their chosen lives. Olive was very aggressive at asking businessmen and city officials for donations, and she became well known among them for her rescue efforts on behalf of these women. Consequently, the city appointed Olive as women's jail matron. Seattle had no women's jail, so Olive took the prisoners into her own home. The women were barricaded into rooms upstairs where Olive sometimes had to administer morphine in small doses to drug-addicted prisoners.

Next, Olive and Noble founded the City Mission Foundling Home as a haven for girls in trouble. The home quickly filled with unwed pregnant girls and prostitutes, and the babies born to them there. The girls all engaged in household chores, changed diapers, and cared for the infants born at the home as part of their rehabilitation. Many of the babies born to these unfortunate mothers died due to malnutrition and disease. There is a potter's field in south Seattle where most are buried. The babies that survived were nursed to health and cared for lovingly by Olive until good homes could be found for them. The young mothers often stayed on at the Ryther Home, helping with the work and acting as older sisters to the younger ones until they found jobs. Olive Ryther had made many contacts with Seattle businessmen through her fund-raising. These contacts proved useful in finding employment for her girls. Those that showed potential went on to business college. Children were also cared for by Mother Ryther while their young mothers worked.

Olive was so successful at nursing the malnourished babies of fallen women to health, that doctors began sending sick babies to her for care. Word spread of her deeds and, before long, babies and children were dropped off at the home by parents unable to care for them. At one time, Mother Ryther had thirteen babies, all under six months of age, in her care.

When the Florence Crittendon Home for Unwed Mothers opened, Olive changed the focus of her work to sheltering destitute and homeless children. The children were well cared for, given love, and educated, but they were also expected to participate in the work of running the home. Older children were encouraged to mentor and care for younger children, and all were treated as members of a large family. If homes had not been found for the children by their teenage years, they were taught a trade.

Olive worked tirelessly, in a house with no plumbing—cooking, sewing, cleaning, gardening, raising livestock to provide food for the ever-hungry mouths, and caring for a home full of babies and children. Mother Ryther refereed fights, nursed sick and injured feelings and bodies, all while continuously managing the home with wisdom and good humor. Asked once by a newspaper reporter how she did it all, Mother Ryther responded, "Oh, that's easy, I like it."

Olive Ryther was constantly appealing to Seattle's citizens for aid. Farmers brought her excess produce and dairy products, local mills donated cereal and flour, and women's groups made clothing for the children. She was not above visiting local businesses and refusing to leave until she received a check. Once, Mother Ryther entered a Seattle store with twenty-five of her children and addressed the proprietor directly, "These children are staying here until you fit them all with shoes—that'll be your contribution to the Ryther Child Home."

One skill Olive Ryther lacked was record keeping. Mother Ryther kept no receipts, records of expenditures, or donations. She was constantly at odds with the city health department at the turn of the century. In 1902, city health officials threatened to close the home for not meeting new codes. Laurence Colman, who built Colman Dock, Seattle's ferry terminal, formed a board of citizens to appeal for funds and support the home. As a result of Colman's efforts, the home was renovated and fitted with electricity and indoor plumbing, efforts which brought the home up to city code.

Businesses and citizens continued to contribute money to the home. Noble, often away working on construction projects, sent his salary to Olive. Additionally, Mother Ryther published a small magazine, "The Orphan," which the children sold as a fund-raiser. Still, there were shortages.

In 1893, the Ryther's daughter Amy was taken by the smallpox epidemic. Then, Mae Bird became crippled with rheumatoid arthritis, and medical bills mounted. In 1905, the mortgage was foreclosed. Laurence Colman came to the rescue again, finding the Rythers a large mansion on Denny Way. The once grand home had fallen into disrepair. Colman was able to secure rent at the rate of one hundred dollars a month, due to the condition of the manor. With her large family, Mother Ryther moved to the Denny Way home. After fifteen years in the mansion, the building began to deteriorate hopelessly. No more repairs would fix the leaky roof and faulty plumbing. A campaign was started to gather funds to find a larger, more modern building for Mother Ryther and her children.

Among the fund-raising efforts for the home was a drive to sell bricks to Seattle citizens. These bricks were then used in the construction of the Ryther Home. The money was raised and in May of 1920, the family moved to their new home on Stoneway Avenue. The *Seattle Post-Intelligence* headline for moving day announced, "Autos Will Transfer Big Family to Its New Home." The home and its occupants were moved in private cars provided by Seattle's caring community.

In 1922, the Ryther Child Home's board pronounced Mother Ryther "too old, dominating, and arbitrary" to run the home. The board members resigned and a new superintendent was appointed to run the Ryther Home. Within three weeks, the superintendent was gone and Mother Ryther back at the helm. Only then did she consent to allowing nurses in to examine and vaccinate the children. Thereafter, several attempts were made to oust Mother Ryther, but the community adored her and staunchly supported her work. In 1930, a reluctant Olive Ryther had to be forced onto a stage at the Pantages Theater to accept an award as "Seattle's Sweetheart."

When she turned eighty in 1929, Mother Ryther was quoted as saying, "I'll never grow old. Most folk grow old as their children grow up. Every time one of my children grows up I have a new youngster to take his place and I have to stay young with my children."

Mother Ryther managed the home on Stoneway for fourteen years until her death at the age of eighty-five on October 2, 1934. Sadly, the once bustling home was silent for an entire year after

Mother Ryther's death. The board wanted the Ryther Child Home to continue as a community service to children and sought a way to do so. The next year, in June of 1935, the School of Social Work at the University of Washington conducted a study, which resulted in a recommendation that the home be converted into a psychiatric service center for children exhibiting "emotional instability or behavior problems." The home was reopened in 1935, as the Ryther Child Center, to be supported entirely by community funds.

The Ryther Child Center operated at the Stoneway house for twenty years before moving to its present location in North Seattle. Children come to the center with a variety of emotional, psychological, and chemical-addiction problems for which they receive loving care and professional treatment. Mother Ryther's philosophy of recognizing each child as an individual—rather than a naughty, troubled youngster—is still followed. Thus, the legacy of Olive Hannah Spore Ryther lives on in Seattle to this day. ⚜

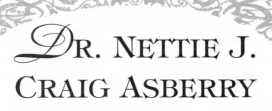

$\mathcal{D}$R. NETTIE J. CRAIG ASBERRY

1865–1968

Doctor of Music/Champion of Civil Rights

$\mathcal{O}$n the occasion of her one-hundredth birthday, Dr. Nettie J. Asberry told reporters that she believed she was the nation's first black woman to receive a doctoral degree for any subject. If only she could locate her diploma, then she would show it to the reporter. The diploma, a Doctorate of Music, presented to Nettie on June 12, 1883, by the Kansas Conservatory of Music and Elocution in Leavenworth, had been neatly framed but was now missing. The distinguished document had been lost in the large old Tacoma home Nettie had lived in for well over fifty years. It was at this address, 1219 South Thirteenth Street, where Nettie taught piano lessons to generations of Tacoma students. "They were of all colors and walks of life, for this has always been a melting pot area of the city." Mrs. Asberry was one of the best known piano teachers in Tacoma.

* * *

Nettie J. Craig was born at the close of the Civil War on July 15, 1865, in Leavenworth, Kansas, to Violet Craig and William Wallingford. Nettie attended school in Leavenworth, where the pu-

Nettie Asberry

pils were segregated by grade level, not race. She began taking piano lessons at age eight, and even then she showed a great aptitude for music.

As a youngster, Nettie had the opportunity to meet Susan B. Anthony who was in town to visit her brother Daniel R. Anthony, publisher of the *Leavenworth Times*. Nettie remained an admirer and, at age thirteen, became secretary of a women's club, the Susan B. Anthony Club.

Nettie decided to attend college at a time when few women, few blacks, and even fewer black women were studying at the university level. It was still "The Reconstruction Era" in the South, the post–Civil War period lasting from 1865-1877, during which the country struggled to reunite. During Reconstruction, new governments in the southern states eliminated racially discriminatory laws and established the first state-supported, free public school systems in the South. The state university was free to all, so Nettie decided to further her education. After she completed her undergraduate work at the University of Kansas, she pursued an advanced degree in music at The Kansas Conservatory of Music and Elocution, a private college in Leavenworth. In 1883, at age eighteen, Nettie Craig received a diploma granting her the "rights, privileges, and dignities" of a doctorate in the teaching of music.

Following college, Nettie J. Craig married Albert Jones. She taught music and performed in church choirs in Kansas City and Denver before moving to the Northwest. News of Seattle's Great Fire in 1889, and the subsequent rebuilding of the city, spread excitement throughout the midwest about new opportunities in Seattle. Nettie and Albert Jones arrived in Seattle by train in 1890 "amid much bustle and excitement. Trains every day were bringing families from all parts of the country. It was a time of friendship and good neighborliness." Nettie Jones became the organist and musical director for the First AME (African Methodist Episcopal) Church.

After Albert Jones's death, Nettie remarried and moved to Tacoma in 1893. Her new husband, Henry J. Asberry, was the well-known owner of the Tacoma Hotel Barbershop. Henry's clients included not only Tacoma's distinguished citizens, but dignitaries including United States presidents. It was the custom, at the time, for patrons to keep shaving mugs bearing their names on a shelf at the barber shop. When Henry Asberry died in 1939, Nettie donated the collection to the Washington State Historical Museum, along with a lace opera coat she had made for the opening of the Seattle-Yukon-Pacific Exposition World's Fair in 1909.

Nettie Asberry became well known in Tacoma, not only as a music teacher, but for her endless civic involvement. One of her many civic endeavors was to serve as president of the Allen Red Cross in Tacoma.

Many improvement clubs for black women in Tacoma were begun at Nettie's hand. All of these clubs became charter members of the Washington State Federation of Colored Women's Organizations, which was formed in 1917. Nettie served as an officer and state statistician for the organization. The purpose of the federation is stated in the preamble to their constitution:

> We, the colored women of the State of Washington and Jurisdiction, feeling the need of united and systematic effort along moral, physical and intellectual lines, in order to elevate our race, do hereby unite into a State Federation.

Although not officially organized until 1917, the activities of the federation began in 1908, with the preparation for Seattle's Alaska-Yukon-Pacific Exposition World's Fair to be held in 1909. An announcement was made that there would be a women's building for display of handicrafts. Nettie Asberry and a group of Tacoma women became inspired with the idea of displaying the work of the black women of Tacoma and Pierce County at the exposition. These women formed the Clover Leaf Art Club for just that purpose. They had one year to work! The women applied for space in the Women's Building and set to work on their handicrafts. In May of 1909, articles created by the women of the Clover Leaf Art Club were on display for the fair's opening day. The exhibit consisted of needlework, oil and watercolor paintings, ceramics, and china painting. Three medals were awarded to the Clover Leaf Art Club: a gold medal for the entire exhibit; a silver medal for the Battenburg lace opera coat valued at $500, which had been made by Nettie Asberry; and, a bronze medal for the paintings and ceramics of Mrs. Hiram Moore-Baker.

After reading about the National Association for the Advancement of Colored People's (NAACP) work on behalf of blacks in the East, Dr. Asberry decided, along with others, to found a branch in Tacoma. Nettie Asberry submitted the group's application to the New York office of the NAACP, and the branch received its charter in 1913. The Tacoma Branch of the NAACP was the first branch formed west of Kansas City. Following the founding of the Tacoma Branch of the NAACP in 1913, the group founded branches in Portland, Seattle, Spokane, and other Northwest cities, including cities in Canada and Alaska.

The Tacoma Branch of the NAACP's first official act was to rally against a measure being considered in the state legislature banning interracial marriages. Someone working in the legislature tipped the group off that this measure was being discussed. Overnight, the Tacoma NAACP Branch organized a caravan of cars including not only Blacks, but Whites, Filipinos, and others. They descended on Olympia's powerful Rules Committee, and in a surprise move, defeated the measure.

In 1961, at age ninety-six, Dr. Nettie Asberry was honored for her outstanding achievements in the field of voluntary social service by the Tacoma City Association of Colored Women. The Asberry Cultural Club, one of the women's groups within the City Association, was named for Nettie. On that occasion, Nettie was interviewed by *The Tacoma News Tribune* and was quoted as saying, "I didn't intend to devote my life to teaching, and after I was no longer young, I turned to social work for which there seemed such an endless need." Mrs. Asberry went on to note that early social work was largely done by volunteers such as herself rather than by paid professionals.

At age ninety-six, Nettie still played her piano and walked daily, as well as conducted activities in business and social affairs. She was a devoted member of the Allen African Methodist Episcopal Church, and of the Baha'i Faith. Baha'i is an organization founded in 1863 in Iran, which emphasizes the spiritual unity and brotherhood of all mankind. Dr. Asberry explained that Baha'i includes intelligent people of all colors and classes. All are welcome except for people who belong to groups that maintain color barriers. She belonged to the Baha'i Faith for over twenty-five years.

During her ninety-sixth birthday interview in 1961, Nettie expressed her views on current events of the time:

> Courage is the saving grace in this tense world racial situation. Courage of the white people who dare to show their fairness by helping us achieve positions of human dignity, and courage of those of other races who risk insults by quietly asserting their rights as human beings. Money fears are at the base of the prejudice—Ministers, who must believe in our cause if their faith is sincere, are afraid to speak out lest they offend some in their congregations and lose their pulpits; school boards in many places, labor organizations which are afraid to open their

doors to colored people lest some white people be put out of work. . . . wherever one goes, it is the same.

Dr. Asberry also blamed uncensored television for the 1960s youth riots and delinquencies of all races. "Some have estimated that ten years will see the ironing out of most racial difficulties. I believe it will take much longer, and I can scarcely believe that I shall not be here to see it. I keep making long-range plans. I don't think any differently than when I was a young woman."

Nettie J. Craig Jones Asberry died in a Tacoma nursing home on November 17, 1968. At age 103, she was one of Tacoma's oldest residents. Even at her advanced age, Nettie cared for and followed young people as she had in her younger years. In 1902, Dr. Asberry had organized the Mozart Musical Club. This society for young people started with the purpose of broadening their musical culture and knowledge of the lives of great composers. In the year of her death, she donated musical instruments and materials to a library and music hall in Tacoma's Hilltop neighborhood. The Youth Auxiliary of the Asberry Cultural Club built and furnished the room which was named in her honor. Thomas Simms, an artist residing on McNeil Island, donated a painting of Nettie for the hall. The hall is still located in the Tacoma City Association of Colored Women's Group Clubhouse on South Yakima Avenue.

In 1969, Tacoma's mayor, A.L. Rasmussen, proclaimed May 11, Dr. Nettie Asberry Day. Money was collected for a city memorial in her honor. Events were held on the campuses of The University of Puget Sound and Tahoma High School.

One thing Dr. Asberry failed to do before she died was to locate her precious diploma. Since she had no children, Nettie's possessions were given or sold to friends and relatives after her death. Most of the items were then stored away. In 1976, during the country's bicentennial celebrations, a Tacoma woman was watching a TV show during which they displayed Abraham Lincoln's actual diplomas. Suddenly it occurred to her that she had seen Nettie Asberry's diploma in the possessions she had obtained from the estate. The discovery came at a time when the Asberry Cultural Club was making plans for Tacoma's Black Bicentennial Celebration. The glass frame was broken and the paper brown and crumpled with age, but nevertheless, it was a priceless find. The diploma was displayed during the bicentennial and was hung permanently next to the painting of Dr. Nettie J. Asberry in the Music Room of the Tacoma City Association of Colored Women's Clubhouse. ⚜

DR. MARY ARCHER LATHAM
1844–1917

Physician–Fugitive

"*Wanted* dead or alive!" So stipulated the warrant issued for the arrest of Dr. Mary A. Latham.

By lying flat in the bed of a wagon, Mary had escaped the detection of the Spokane County Sheriff as she was driven out of town. As soon as the wagon passed the city limits, Mary climbed up next to her driver where she remained seated for the rest of the ride to her home in the town of Mead, Washington. Once in Mead, she gathered together a few belongings, hitched up her own horse and buggy, and lit out for the Idaho border, with the sheriff's posse in pursuit.

Dr. Latham's successful escape was due to the aid of countless friends throughout Spokane County and Idaho—friends she had made while practicing medicine in the Inland Northwest for nearly twenty years.

*   *   *

Mary Archer* was born November 5, 1844, in New Richmond, Ohio, to Jane (Warren) Archer and English-born James Ar-

---

* Mary's Death Certificate lists her maiden name as Archer; her obituary lists the name as Archard.

Dr. Mary Archer Latham

cher. She was educated at the Claremont Academy in Claremontville, Ohio. On July 28, 1864, Mary Archer married prominent physician Dr. Edward H. Latham. The couple had three sons: Frank, James, and Warren. Like most women of her day, Mary devoted herself to her family as a young wife. As her sons grew, Mary—a woman of high energy—desired more, and following in her husband's footsteps, she entered medical school when she was in her late thirties. At the Miami Medical College in Cincinnati, Ohio, Mary Latham was a member of the first class of women students allowed into the clinical wards of the Cincinnati General Hospital.

In 1884, at the age of forty, Mary was granted her medical degree. For three years, she practiced medicine in Cincinnati before she and her husband decided to move west. They had grown tired of the harsh Ohio winters and sought a milder climate in the Pacific Northwest. They migrated west to Spokane from Ohio in late 1887 or early 1888. In Spokane, Mary Latham earned the gratitude not only of her patients for skillful, loving care, but of the entire community for her extensive devotion to civic service.

Dr. Mary Latham's practice in Spokane flourished, as did the ever expanding population of the city of Spokane. She is believed to be the first woman physician to practice medicine in the state of Washington, although the state did not begin licensing physicians until 1921. Female doctors were a rarity at the time; for those few women that did practice medicine, the acceptable specialty was in the diseases of women and children. Following that convention, Mary began a practice treating women and children. In a January 1, 1892, *Spokane Spokesman* article, Mary's practice is described, ". . . her business has grown with the marvelous growth of the city, and in her special line of work—the diseases of women and children—she has no superior in the State." She was regarded as one of the foremost medical practitioners, male or female, in Washington. For many years Mary had the most lucrative medical practice of any woman in the state.

Mary dedicated her practice to alleviating the pain and suffering of her patients. One of her patients, an author, made the following book dedication to Mary.

I owe this to you for your love shown to me in my sickness and sorrow and despair. Many times when hope had almost vanished you came to me with that sweet womanly sympathy, so cheering and encouraging, and if this book ever proves a blessing to the public or me, we can turn with grateful hearts to you.

Standing 5' 6" tall, erect of carriage, with brown hair, blue eyes, and angular features, Mary exuded dignity, pride, and professionalism. Mary Latham was a consummate female professional in a world which regarded this as a novelty.

Dr. Mary A. Latham's medical skills were widely recognized. She was elected unanimously to a professorship of obstetrics at the innovative new medical school, the Washington Biochemic Medical College, which was established in Spokane by Dr. George W. Carey in 1889. She served as chairman of the Medical Department for the Washington Branch of the Queen Isabelle Association at the World's Columbian Exposition. Described in a newspaper as "the crowning glory of her work" was a women's hospital built for Dr. Latham in Spokane's Lidgerwood District in 1892. Mary not only ran the Lidgerwood Women's Hospital but headed and managed the Spokane Children's Home. However, her compassion was not limited to just humans, as Dr. Latham also acted as secretary and treasurer of Spokane's Humane Society.

Edward and Mary Latham were separated within a few months of their arrival in Spokane, in June of 1888. After thirty-one years of marriage, the couple divorced on July 18, 1895. Dr. Edward Latham left Spokane to serve as a government physician for twenty-five years in Nespelem, on the Colville Indian Reservation. Independently, Mary carried on her practice and community work in Spokane.

Mary Archer Latham was a proud woman, with endless ideas, dedication, and energy directed not only toward her medical profession, but toward many civic activities. Her motto in practicing medicine was "progress." To this end, she was also identified with many progressive movements in the growing city of Spokane.

Dr. Latham was the driving force behind the creation of Spokane's first public library in 1894. Prior to that time, the city harbored a few small private reading libraries which Mary had helped to found. Mary was also a promoter and director of a reading room owned and operated by Spokane's labor unions. Dr. Latham suggested merging the private libraries and the Union Reading Room to create a larger public facility. To accomplish this, Mary Latham and a handful of others personally rang doorbells throughout the city in an effort to collect books for the new library. The new City Library was also privileged to receive a set of encyclopedias donated by Mary from her own private library.

In her spare time, Mary took up writing. She began by writing stories for local newspapers and magazines. Then she translated a story from German for a leading magazine and eventually published a novel, *A Witch's Wreath,* in the 1890s. One reviewer described the novel as, "written in the author's usually forcible style, [it] is decidedly realistic, and will be a masterpiece of fiction."

This multitalented lady was described in a Spokane daily paper of the early 1890s:

In nearly every community there is one who is mediator between wretchedness and wealth, a person whom the affluent respect and the needy love, a person who preserves the rays of summer to dispel the gloom of winter, one who condemns wrong, but pities the wrong-doer, one who has sentiment without sentimentalism, shrewdness without cynicism, dignity without haughtiness, one whose heart pities the suffering, but does not confine that pity to an imaginary field of action, one who believes in human nature, whose nature has not been soured by disappointments, who is too liberal to heartily espouse a creed or sect or religion, who conciliates all doctrines in universal good will to all—such a character is Dr. Mary A. Latham. Probably no woman in all Washington has so many friends as she. Many of the poor into whose lives she has thrown sunshine regard her as their patron saint.

A fellow doctor said of her, "I believe that Mrs. Latham's career, brilliant as it has been in this city, is only in its beginning, for with her indomitable energy she will go on until the highest success is hers."

So, what happened to the brilliant career of this woman of boundless energy, empathy, and creativity? What could have caused this upstanding doctor to become a fugitive from justice—a convicted felon running from a sheriff's posse to avoid a prison sentence? How does such an outstanding, well-respected community member fall so far?

Mary's troubles began in April of 1903, when her adult son James, who had been living with her, was killed. James, a brakeman for Northern Pacific, was crushed between two train cars he was attempting to uncouple. Additionally, Mary suffered a stroke, which left her partially paralyzed and walking with a pronounced limp.

Like many women of her day, Dr. Latham never cared for living alone. After James's death, Mary deeded a store she had purchased in the town of Mead to James's fiancée, Jennie Johnson, on the condition that Jennie live with Dr. Latham at her home in Mead. When Jennie failed to hold up her end of the contract, Mary felt she was being cheated and attempted to reclaim the title to the store by deeding it to a third party. The end result was a lawsuit which lasted a year and ended in a victory for Miss Johnson. According to witnesses, Dr. Latham stated that Jennie would never possess the store. On May 7, 1905, shortly after the litigation ended, the Mead store was burned to the ground by an act of arson.

Dr. Mary A. Latham was arrested and charged with the crime of arson. She pled not guilty to the charge. A case against her was built from circumstantial evidence, including the fact that she was seen watching the fire burn late at night, that she had moved her possessions from the store prior to the fire, and that she had allegedly attempted to create false alibis for the night in question. Dr. Mary A. Latham was found guilty by a jury of her peers on June 18, 1905.

Before her sentencing, Mary was free on bond. Her son's death, the betrayal of his fiancée, and the civil and criminal trials took their toll on Mary's mental health. On June 30, 1905, days before she was to be sentenced for the arson, Mary had an emotional breakdown in the streets of Spokane. While riding a streetcar through the heart of the city, she began wailing and carrying on about going to meet her deceased son, James. Mary was taken into custody for her own protection and had to be carried into court on a stretcher for her sentencing.

The sentencing for the arson verdict took place before Judge Miles Poindexter on July 20, 1905, after her motion for a trial de novo (a new trial) had been denied. Dr. Mary A. Latham was sentenced to four years in prison and ordered to pay fines and court fees in excess of fifteen hundred dollars. Mary, still proclaiming her innocence, appealed her case to the Washington Supreme Court and remained free on bond pending appeal.

Devastated by the sentence, Mary fled the state of Washington. A *Seattle Post-Intelligencer* headline read, "Dr. Latham Flees in Open Buggy—Sheriff Asked to Catch Spokane Fugitive Either Dead or Alive." The sheriff of Spokane County and his posse pursued a relentless search for the doctor for two weeks before they located and arrested her in the mountains of northern Idaho. The fugitive, Mary Latham, was returned to the confines of the Spokane County Jail until January 9, 1906, when she was transferred to the Washington State Penitentiary at Walla Walla. Her attorney, D. W. Henley, wrote to Governor Mead in July of 1906, asking him to pardon Mary. The petition was denied. Mary Latham served one year and three months of her four-year sentence. On April 1, 1907, Mary was paroled from the State Penitentiary to the supervision of her son, Frank.

During her parole, Mary wrote a letter dated May 22, 1907, asking Walla Walla prison warden, M.F. Kincaid, for permission to resume the practice of medicine:

> "Many old friends and many new ones are anxious for me to do so. My home of course would be still with my son and everything [would] be in keeping with the conditions of my parole. But I could then be able to cumulate a sum of money, which I very much need as my pretend friends, lawyers et al. have robbed me unmercifully."

The warden's response was, "Tell her she may do so *with pleasure.*"

Dr. Mary A. Latham began practicing medicine once again in an office adjacent to a drug store owned, in part, by her son. Although her career had been interrupted by her trial and incarceration, Mary was practicing medicine up until the time of her death.

While nursing a twelve-day-old infant stricken with pneumonia, Mary contracted pneumonia herself. The baby and Mary passed away within a day of each other. Dr. Latham died at Sacred Heart Hospital in Spokane on January 20, 1917, at the age of seventy-two.

Remembered as a pioneer woman physician of great civic involvement, Dr. Mary A. Latham is still well respected for her accomplishments and all else seems to have been forgotten. ⚜

THEA CHRISTIANSEN FOSS

1857–1927

The Original "Tugboat Annie"

"Creak, splash—creak, splash," the rhythmic sound of oars grinding against their locks, then dipping into the waters of the sound caught her attention. The young woman, gutting a fish on the porch of her rough-hewn houseboat, looked up to see a lone rower approaching. Thea had just purchased a salmon from an Indian fisherman on Tacoma's waterfront and was busily at work preparing it for the evening meal. Usually her husband, Andrew, provided fish for the family, but he was across Puget Sound on a carpentry job.

"Hello there," the man called out as he drew near the floating home. "This boat's for sale, would you be interested?"

"How much?" asked the woman in her thick Norwegian accent.

"Ten dollars," came the reply.

Thea considered the offer carefully. Ten dollars was a lot of money to the Foss family. Money was scarce, but she was so tired of hauling heavy buckets of water on foot from the creek that emptied into the bay a quarter mile from her home. "I'll give you five dollars," countered the astute Thea Foss.

Thea Christiansen Foss

"Okay," the rower responded to her amazement, "I'm leaving town anyway and have no further use for the boat."

The rustic appearance of the houseboat must have tipped the seller that money was a rare commodity in the Foss household, and perhaps he took pity on Thea in accepting her offer.

When Andrew Foss returned home two months later, he proudly pulled out his earnings, pouring thirty-two dollars worth of gold and silver coins onto the kitchen table. Without a word, Thea extracted the contents of her cookie jar, forty dollars. Then, to her dumbfounded husband she remarked in Norwegian, "I sell and rent rowboats. No matter what time of the day or night people come for them, I am always ready!"

That hot summer night in 1889, Thea's purchase of the rowboat gave birth to the Foss Maritime Company, the largest towing, barging, and marine transportation services operation in the Northwest and one of the largest in the United States. The company motto, coined by Thea Christiansen Foss, is "Always Ready!"

With a remarkably intuitive business sense, Thea knew that there would be a demand for rowboats. She adorned her five-dollar purchase with green and white paint, colors that would become well known in Northwest waters, and sold the boat for a profit. Next, she bought two more boats, which she repainted and resold, buying four boats. Soon Thea had her own fleet of rowboats which she rented out to fishermen and duck hunters for 25 to 50 cents a day. Thea Foss's head for business, coupled with her husband's shipbuilding and maritime skills, soon built the Fosses a fleet of 200 rowboats. Henry Foss, the couple's youngest son, described his parents in a 1966 interview, "Mother was absolutely honest but shrewd. Father was not strong physically, but he was always ready to help anyone out—day or night."

* * *

Thea Christiansen was born on June 8, 1857, in Eidsberg, Norway. While visiting her sister, Julia, and brother-in-law, Theodore, in Christiana (now Oslo), Thea met Andrew Olesen, the seafaring brother of Theodore, whose ship happened to be in port. Andrew was attracted to the proud young woman, with her golden braids coiled neatly upon her head. The young mariner could not read or write, but his strong goals and idealistic visions appealed to Thea.

Andrew's dream had always been to sail across the Atlantic Ocean. He and Thea made plans for a future home in the promised land of America. Andrew shipped out, working as a forecastle hand on a vessel bound for Quebec. From Canada, Andrew went south to Saint Paul, Minnesota, drawn by its large Norwegian community. Instead of working with his beloved boats, Andrew found a job building houses and saved every penny to send for his fiancée.

Finally, when he had saved enough for her passage, Andrew sent money to Thea. To his surprise, his brother, Iver, showed up in Saint Paul instead. Andrew set to work earning more money to send for his intended. When he had again sent enough money for Thea's trip to America, he was greeted by his sister, Kristina. Frustrated, Andrew now intended to go to Norway and fetch Thea himself! Before he could do this, Thea arrived in Minnesota of her own volition. Determined to pay her own passage to America, she had given the money Andrew sent her to his family members. Thea had worked as an indentured servant to a wealthy family until she had earned enough for her way over. Andrew and Thea were married in St. Paul, Minnesota, in 1882.

St. Paul's Norwegian community already had so many Olesens that Andrew and Thea changed their last name to Olesen-Fossen, the latter meaning waterfall. As the family became more Americanized they shortened their surname to Foss.

During the eight years the Fosses lived in Minnesota, three children were added to the family: Arthur in 1885, Wedell in 1887, and Lillian in 1889. A daughter, Lilly Marie, was also born in Minnesota, but died at age four.

Andrew's love for the sea and strong dislike of cold winters would lead the family west to Tacoma, Washington, on the waters of Commencement Bay in Puget Sound. Leaving his young family, Andrew ventured into the Northwest in 1888. He worked his way west as a carpenter for the Northern Pacific Railroad and, once in Tacoma, became employed as a deck hand for the Tacoma Tugboat Company. In his spare time, Andrew combed beaches for cedar logs with which to build a floating house. Beached logs and salvaged timber were crafted into a simple, one-room floathouse for his family. When finished, the house contained a secondhand stove, beds, a table, and some crude furniture.

After being separated for eight months, Thea and the children traveled aboard an immigrant train to meet Andrew in Tacoma. The end of each railcar held a stove, and the air was thick with greasy smoke from cooking. The train was noisy, sooty, and packed full of immigrant families. Thea arrived in Tacoma in the spring of 1889, near exhaustion from caring for three children—all under the age of five (including one newborn baby)—aboard the crowded, grimy train.

With pride, Andrew brought his young family directly from the train station to their new floating home. A rough-slabbed, wooden structure with a tarpaper roof and stark furnishings floated before her, but seeing her husband's pride, Thea could show no disappointment. She viewed the situation as temporary and accepted her lot even though she would have to haul fresh water to the houseboat every day. Thea could not have imagined then that the family would live on Tacoma's waterfront for nearly a quarter of a century. That

FOSS MARITIME COMPANY, SEATTLE, WA

Original Foss float house in 1890. Andrew and Thea are on the deck with Lillian in Thea's arms.

first day, both of her young boys added to her apprehension by falling into the bay. Though she harbored a fear of the water, which she never overcame, Andrew's enthusiasm and the natural beauty of their Puget Sound surroundings soon won over Thea Foss.

Once settled into her new home, the young wife's hands were full with housekeeping, washing, and caring for three small children aboard a floating home with no running water. Within three weeks of the family's arrival, Thea became very sick, and for three months she battled typhoid-pneumonia. Andrew begged a local doctor to come to the houseboat and treat his deathly ill wife. The kind doctor paid the houseboat call and provided Thea with medicine at no cost. Although the Fosses could not pay the doctor's fee then, they never forgot the kindness. In more prosperous years, they made substantial donations to Tacoma hospitals. As Thea recovered, Andrew's health began to falter, a fact he blamed on the cold Minnesota winters he had endured.

With Thea expecting a fourth child and Andrew beginning employment anew at a shipyard, the family was forced to move. The city of Tacoma was diverting the Puyallup River to promote industrial development. The Fosses moved their tiny wooden houseboat to "Hallelujah Harbor," named for the Salvation Army shacks dotting the shoreline. Water would still have to be hauled into their home.

In search of more income for his family, Andrew took a construction job on the Kitsap Peninsula across Puget Sound. He would have to be away from his family for two months. It was during this time that Thea launched the family business with the purchase of the five-dollar rowboat. Thea's timing was impeccable; sport boating was extremely popular, thus the business flourished. A sign bearing the slogan, "Always Ready," was posted on the roof of the floathouse. The floating home bustled with activity and thrived as a business. This enabled Andrew to enjoy his chosen vocation, boat building, to add to their fleet.

With the birth of another son, Henry, in 1891, the family now counted six members and had outgrown their tiny floathouse. Andrew and his two oldest sons built a larger houseboat in another saltwater location. This house had a modern amenity—running water! The Foss floating home became a center for Norwegian social activities, as well as for the Foss boating business. Thea was hospitable by nature and loved to entertain the local Norwegian community at "kaffe slaberas" (coffee klatches) in her spacious new home.

Although Thea loved her rowboat rental business, Andrew felt driven to create more. Using the old houseboat as a workshop, he and his brothers salvaged parts from a wrecked steamboat and built a fifty-foot steamer. They lost money on the unsuccessful venture but thought they were on to something.

The young Foss boys spent the majority of their time on the beach. Thea, still deathly afraid of the water, at first tried to keep them away from it. Later, she gave in and let them follow the lure of the sea. Soon the children were venturing forth on the sound by boat. The boys helped build the boats, bailed and cleaned the returned rentals, gave sailing lessons, and collected spilled bait from the rental boats and resold it to fishermen. Thea's enterprising sons even developed their own business by beginning a rescue operation with their powerboat. Using a telescope, they searched for boaters in distress. They did not charge to rescue their own customers, but if the boaters had not rented from the Fosses, they were charged twenty-five cents.

One day, it dawned on Thea that her boys could run an efficient ship-to-shore delivery service. She purchased a two-horsepower launch, reasoning that the ships anchored in the sound would be better served by the small powerboat than by the rowboats presently bringing them supplies. This acquisition became the first of many powerboats owned by the "Foss Launch Company." Andrew set to work building more boats, and before long they had Foss launches serving every ship in the harbor.

The Foss Launch Company did so well that they were able to buy a fleet of launches from a competitor and ultimately take on the bulk of the harbor service and ship docking on Puget Sound. The Fosses continued to service the anchored ships in Puget Sound, bringing supplies, fresh food, and a water-taxi service to the crews. The boys' tactic was to meet incoming ships with a box of Washington apples and pitch their company's services.

Thea's boys would go on to lifelong careers in boating with the family business. Her daughters would not live to see the family business at its peak. Thea's second to last child, Lela, was stillborn, and her four-year-old, Lilly Marie, had died in Minnesota. In 1914,

Thea lost her lovely twenty-five-year-old daughter, Lillian, to tuberculosis. Always accepting, Thea endured Lillian's passing but never recovered fully from the loss. She poured her energy even more fervently into the Foss family business.

Many of Thea's relatives arrived from Norway and became involved in the family business. By the early 1900s, the company had outgrown its headquarters and staff of family members. The Fosses began hiring nonrelated, Scandinavian immigrants, plentiful in the Northwest at the time. Andrew built a dormitory for the growing crew. Thea cooked for twenty-five to thirty men, who dined with the family. She also served as counselor and surrogate mother to the crews. Andrew and Thea insisted the men study for their citizenship tests and become U.S. citizens. The crews rewarded them with loyalty, calling them "Mother and Father Foss."

The Foss general store, run by Thea, supplied ships with food and gear. She stocked the store with fresh eggs, meat, and milk from her own animals, which were kept on an adjacent sandlot. The waterfront store was a popular gathering place among sailors, crews, and dock workers. People were drawn to Thea in spite of her quiet nature. A natural diplomat, this was a woman who had the ability to converse with all of those who frequented the waterfront. These abilities earned her the respect of sea captains, prominent businessmen, dignitaries, and domestic and foreign crews. She ran the boarding house, store, and company office and still had time for her beloved Norwegian Church, as well as for works of charity. She often provided comfort and shelter to young Norwegian immigrant girls. Her philosophy is evident in the following entry of January 19, 1907, from her diary:

> The law imprinted in all men's hearts is to love one another. I will look on the whole world as my Country and all men as my brothers. We are made for cooperation and

to act against one another is to act contrary to nature. Say not I will love the wise and hate the unwise, you should love all mankind. Let us not love in word and in tongue, but in deed and in truth.

Thea Foss had endless stamina with which to perform the multitude of tasks and businesses she undertook. She also had the ability to organize those around her. Each member of the family had multiple chores—even the cow, Annie, had extra duties. Thea kept forty chickens, several pigs, and the cow (which was fed pancakes through the kitchen window). In addition to providing milk, Annie guided boats in dense Pacific fog. When a captain had trouble navigating Puget Sound waters in the heavy fog, he would blow his horn until Annie met the ship at the end of the Fosses' pier with a resounding "Moooo!" She was then paid by the arriving sea captains who, once safely docked, rewarded her with bovine treats.

The turn of the century brought major changes to the Foss Launch Company. Bicycles became the rage, and pleasure rowing was suddenly out of fashion. Automobiles soon replaced travel by rowing and sailing on Puget Sound, and ships became self-propelled, relegating the Foss rowboats and launches to little use.

The Fosses saw the hills all around the Northwest booming with logging activities. These logs were rafted and towed to local mills around the sound. Seizing another opportunity, the Fosses had their launches begin towing rafts of logs, but they lacked the power to do so efficiently. They decided to invest in more powerful engines for their boats. Key to their success was the fact that Thea and Andrew never borrowed for these upgrades. They saved during prosperous times, for they knew their business was cyclical.

The improved boats were better, but Andrew set out to design a boat just for log towing. Andrew designed his tugs by hand carving prototypes. He fashioned a "teardrop"-shaped boat with a more balanced rudder. His concepts became industry standards, though he never patented any of his inventions, saying they were for "the common good." The tug business grew, along with charter hauling of landfill and war cargo during World War I.

In August of 1919, at the close of the War, Thea's sons sponsored a water sports carnival in her honor. August was chosen as the anniversary of her first rowboat purchase and the founding of Foss Launch and Tug Company. The carnival was held at the family's houseboat along Tacoma's waterfront and was attended by hundreds of spectators.

As Thea and Andrew aged, the boys took command of the company. Together, the family had decided that Arthur would leave school in the eighth grade to assist with the growing family business. They later decided that Wedell should attend law school, and Henry business college. Henry was eventually elected to office as a Washington state senator. Throughout her life, Thea worked tirelessly on behalf of the Foss company. In her later years, she continued to help with the business when she could, telling her children, *"Ya, jeg har so mange ting ot gjore."* ("Yes, I have so many things to do yet.") Her interest in Foss Launch and Tug never waned. By now, Andrew had built her a grand house on dry land, uptown where Tacoma's "better people" lived. Unfortunately, the new home was out of sight of the family's fleet of tugs and launches, but her boys always kept her up-to-date on the company. Thea Christiansen Foss passed away on June 7, 1927, one day before her seventieth birthday.

Thea's funeral procession was the largest ever seen in Tacoma. The Foss fleet flew their green and white flags at half-mast as they cruised up Tacoma's waterway. On September 15, 1989, sixty-two years after her death, the Tacoma City Waterway was renamed the Thea Foss Waterway in her honor.

With her son Wedell's assistance, Seattle native Norman Reilly

Raine penned a series based on the life of Thea Foss for the *Saturday Evening Post*. Wedell provided the storyline for the first article, published in 1931. The series ran for some time until Raine began to write scripts for the movie industry. Inspired by Thea's life, Raine wrote the script for the film *Tugboat Annie*. The movie, starring Maureen O'Sullivan, Marie Dressler, and Wallace Beery, premiered in 1933. It was shot on Seattle's Lake Union, Elliott Bay, and throughout the Straits of Juan De Fuca. Although pleased by the tribute, Wedell was quick to point out that the raucous Irish character, "Tugboat Annie," was nothing like his quiet, pious, Norwegian mother with her morbid fear of the water. ⚜

JUDGE REAH MARY WHITEHEAD

1883–1972

Lady Justice

*T*he frightened young man, hardly more than a boy at age nineteen, stood before the bench accused of kidnapping. His voice quavered as he addressed the judge. The sixteen-year-old "victim" sobbed incessantly in the courtroom galley, as her stern father glowered over her toward the accused.

The judge intuitively sensed there was more to this situation than first met the eye and further interviewed the two youths. They had been trying to elope, when the girl's father intervened, charging his daughter's suitor with kidnapping. Finding no criminal intent, Judge Whitehead then conferred with the girl's mother. The magistrate convinced the mother to sign a consent, so the two lovers could be married. The young couple was then married by the compassionate judge.

Every year, on the anniversary of their wedding, the couple phoned Judge Whitehead and updated her on the chronicles of their family life. These calls continued for over fifty years.

It was in October of 1914 that the young assistant King County Prosecutor announced her intention of running for the office of Justice of the Peace for the Precinct of Seattle. Her mother, Mrs.

Judge Whitehead

Esther T. Bosley, managed the campaign. With the backing of a number of prominent male lawyers and judges in Seattle, Reah Mary Whitehead beat out the competition of nine men to become the state of Washington's first female judge. She served on the bench in Seattle for nearly twenty-seven years.

* * *

Reah Mary Whitehead was born April 11, 1883, in Kansas City, Missouri, to Stanley and Esther (Gideon) Whitehead. As a youngster, she moved with her family to Seattle in 1890. She began her legal career as a stenographer. At age sixteen, Reah took a position in a law office in Skagway, Alaska. Living and working in Alaska for fourteen months, Reah became well known as the youngest court reporter in the Alaska Territory.

After mastering her stenographic skills, she reached the point at which she felt she must either go downhill or move forward. It was then she decided to study law, and she enrolled in the University of Washington's School of Law. At least, she reasoned, she would learn what she was writing about when she copied briefs. During her final year of law school, Reah attended evening classes while working days for a Seattle law firm. Reah graduated from law school at the University of Washington and passed the Washington State Bar exam in May of 1905.

Even after passing the bar, Reah did not work as an attorney for several years. She worked for Judge Thomas Burke and then as chief clerk in the King County Prosecutor's Office under Chief Prosecutor MacKintosh. When George F. Vandervear assumed the office of chief prosecutor on January 12, 1909, he appointed Reah M. Whitehead as the first woman prosecutor for King County, as well as for the state of Washington. An article in the *Seattle Post-Intelligencer* noted her appointment, stating that although she has authority to try cases the same as other deputy prosecutors . . . Miss Whitehead will remain as clerk in the office of the prosecuting attorney and will not draw salary as a deputy prosecuting attorney. She will hold the title, however, and is the first woman to be appointed a deputy prosecuting attorney in this state.

Miss Whitehead once prosecuted a cruelty to animals case in the Superior Court and secured a conviction. She will be given an opportunity of handling cases of this character, but for the most part will do office work.

Her duties, as outlined in the article, were quite reflective of the attitudes of the day. Reah Whitehead had to fight an uphill battle toward receiving equal treatment and the same type of caseloads as male prosecutors. Every case which Reah was given the opportunity to try in superior court she won. On this record and the platform of female magistrates for female "culprits," Reah M. Whitehead was elected Justice of the Peace for the Seattle District Court for King County, Washington.

Reah was often described in sexist terms. The local newspaper's description of the ceremony swearing in the state's first female judge began with a fashion statement:

Dressed in a simple blue suit, her brown hair arranged in schoolgirl fashion and her customary rosy cheeks made rosier by the excitement of the occasion, Miss Reah M. Whitehead entered upon her new duties as justice of the peace shortly before noon yesterday morning.

This was hardly a description befitting the decorum of the office! Asked how she liked her new job, she replied, "I will be glad when the novelty of my appearance upon the bench wears off, and I can work like any other justice." A further sign of the times, this article appeared next to an article entitled, "Home Life Regarded as Best for Girls." Even after twenty-seven years of service on the judicial bench, a local columnist interviewing Judge Whitehead asked her for her favorite recipe!

Civil cases tried before Judge Whitehead had a value limitation of one hundred dollars. Every weekday she presided over cases involving laborers' wage claims, creditors holding unpaid promissory notes, landlords due back rent, and auto collision damage. These actions were not so different from those heard in our small claims courts of today.

In October of 1915, a reporter for the *Seattle Post-Intelligencer* newspaper interviewed Judge Whitehead following her first nine months on the bench. He observed, "She looks more like a debutante. Her cheeks are too pink and she's altogether too pretty for a woman judge." Even though the reporter found that he (like most reporters) "could not reconcile her youthful appearance with the dusty, snuffy technicalities of the court room," Judge Whitehead made profound statements in this interview stating:

> [y]ou must remember that for years and years and hundreds of years men have made the laws and men have passed on the interpretation of the man-made laws. Until women have an actual hand in the framing of the laws, make their influence felt in the making of laws, the point of view between men and women judges and men and women lawyers will be different: . . . . I believe, of course, that women should have a hand in making the laws and interpreting them.

Within a year of being sworn in, Judge Whitehead had already heard approximately 1,000 civil cases and 570 criminal cases. Lawyers who practiced before her expressed satisfaction with "the administration of justice by a woman."

Emphasizing the need for women judges, Reah gave an example of a parallel situation, "A few years ago we would not think of having women in police work, yet who would want to go back to that state of things now? They have answered the question of their necessity in the work."

During one of her campaigns for re-election to the bench, Reah further stated:

> There is no sex in brains.
>
> I didn't originate that statement, I simply adopted it in setting forth my belief that a woman is just as mentally capable as a man and that the State of Washington and King County in particular should have a woman superior court judge to even up matters.
>
> Don't get the idea that I think that I or any other woman can do judicial work better than a man. That's just the point at issue. It's that a woman's viewpoint plus a man's viewpoint equals the human viewpoint. And that is what our courts need.

For a 1926 newspaper article, Reah wrote, "Women are still in their infancy in the practice of law." The first woman to practice law in the United States was Myra Bradwell, in Illinois, in 1869. Subsequently, the federal census gave the number of women lawyers in the United States in 1890, as 208; in 1910, as 558; and, in 1920, as 1,738. Judge Whitehead's article also noted that the 1920 census counted male lawyers, judges, and justices in Washington State as 2,208 while females numbered 29. This worked out to a ratio of one male lawyer for every 220 males in the work force; as opposed to one female lawyer for every 3,200 female workers.

There were six Washington women attorneys in public office in 1926: one state senator, one city attorney, two justices of the peace, one deputy prosecuting attorney, and one police judge. The first three positions listed were elective while the last two were appointive. All, with the exception of one, had received their legal training at the University of Washington.

In the 1920s, statistics showed that five years after entering the legal profession, only ten to fifteen percent of male attorneys remained in the active practice of law. Justice Whitehead believed that, "[m]atrimony seems to exert about an equal pressure upon men and women lawyers in separating them from their profession. A young lawyer with matrimony in view recently announced he was going to procure a divorce from the law on the ground of non-support." Apparently, for men, the practice of law was not always the most lucrative profession they could choose. Women, with limited career choices, found the opposite to be true. Reah reported that two former teachers-turned-lawyers claimed they were earning more money than they have ever earned or could have earned in the teaching profession.

Justice Whitehead was chosen as the representative from Washington State to attend a prestigious meeting of professional women in New York City. The American Women's Association invited one woman from each state and the District of Columbia (a total of forty-nine) to attend the 1926 meeting, planned as a tribute to business and professional women of America. Each state delegate was selected by their congressmen, local newspapers, and women's groups.

At age forty-eight, Reah married retired grocer Frank Sidney Harrison. The June, 1931, ceremony was performed by Judge Whitehead's good friend Judge Blanche Funk Miller, a justice of the peace from Tacoma. Reah promised to love and honor her new husband, but the word "obey" was conspicuously absent from the traditional wedding vows. Her announcement that she would continue to use her maiden name for professional reasons met with shock from some in the community. The couple later divorced, and Frank died in 1955.

In 1936, a proposal to reinstate the public whipping post as a means of punishing criminals in Washington State brought strenuous objection from Judge Whitehead. She argued that the whipping post was a testimonial to society's failure to think out problems calmly and clearly, describing the whipping post as an antiquated procedure which does nothing to treat social evils or aid in the correction of criminals. Rather, Justice Whitehead opined, it represented punishment for revenge, with no effort to reduce the cause of crime.

Judge Whitehead served seven terms on the bench in the Precinct of Seattle for King County, Washington. Nearing her retirement, she reflected on the commotion caused by her election in 1914, when, as the newspaper reporter interviewing her noted, "At that time she was pretty nearly the first woman judge in the country, and 'the publicity was terrific.' "Reah laughingly rejected the reporter's suggestion that, in 1941, a woman judge was still a novelty, responding, "[T]here are women sitting on the bench all over the country. I guess it would take the appointment of a woman to the United States Supreme Court to cause a stir any more."*

Judge Whitehead was held in high regard by her fellow attorneys. Wisdom, understanding, and common sense prevailed in her judgments. Her manner consisted of quiet judicial dignity, combined with a polite, but businesslike demeanor.

Reah also took an active interest in promoting legislation for the welfare of women and children. Esther Bosley, Reah's mother, was the driving force behind the funding of the Women's Industrial

---

*An event which was not to occur until 1981, when Justice Sandra Day O'Connor was appointed to the United States Supreme Court.

Home and Clinic in Medical Lake, Washington. As a social worker, Esther saw the need for a correctional school for delinquent adult women. Esther organized support for the project from state social welfare agencies, and Reah drafted the bill. The measure was presented to the state legislature where it passed, with funding granted for two years.

With her husband, Frank, Reah lived in a grand old manor, once a rectory, which had been moved during the Denny Regrade, when Seattle's steepest hills were sluiced away. Weekends were spent at her summer cabin on Lake Sammamish. In the summer, she commuted from her lake home, "as much as her work would allow." A frequent walker, Judge Reah Whitehead was known to walk from downtown Seattle to Ballard or up Queen Anne Hill, round trip distances of twelve and eight miles respectively. Rhea loved Seattle, claiming, "the air here is something to be found nowhere else in the world. It's a mixture of the tang of the sea, that rare air from the mountains and earthy smell of cedar and fir."

When she retired on November 10, 1941, citing health reasons, she was replaced by Evangeline Starr, an attorney who had been appointed Divorce Proctor for the King County Prosecutor's Office by Chief Prosecutor Warren G. Magnuson. Magnuson ("Maggie") later served six terms in the United States Senate, becoming nationally known for his power and influence.

Judge Reah M. Whitehead passed away at age eighty-nine, on October 13, 1972. She had been residing in California with her niece at the time of her death. Her obituary listed her as one of the first women lawyers in the state and Seattle's first female judge. ⚜

MAUDE C. LILLIE BOLIN
1891–1966

Yakama Cowgirl Aviator

*F*ingers tightly clenching the plane's doorway as her clothing was whipped about by the wind, the dark-haired, young woman summoned up her courage and leapt from the airplane. Free falling downward toward the earth, Maude pulled at her parachute cord. The chute opened, stopping her plunge with an abrupt jerk. She then enjoyed the pleasant experience of drifting through space to the ground. "I don't think I'll take another jump soon unless it becomes necessary, but I certainly enjoyed the sensation of the two trial jumps," Maude assessed.

Maude made two such parachute jumps as a prerequisite to receiving her pilot's license. Learning to fly in 1927, just nine years after Amelia Earhart began flying, Maude was one of Washington State's early female aviators. She was one of only two women living in the Yakima Valley to pilot a plane solo, and the first American Indian woman (a member of the Yakama Tribe) in the state, and probably the country, to fly.

Her first attempt to fly solo was one of Maude's biggest thrills. She described how difficult it was for a beginner to hold a plane steady but, finally, she learned to handle the control stick. Making a

LOWELL EVANS, TOPPENISH, WA

Maude C. Lillie Bolin

good landing was her hardest problem. Still, she persevered until she was able to bring her plane to earth without serious jolts or "zooms."

Maude loved flying, participating in air shows and cross-country flights. In 1928, Maude made her first cross-country flight. With another pilot, she flew across the country dropping campaign literature for Senator C.C. Dill. A charter member of the Yakima Lady Birds, a woman's aviation club formed in 1928, she endeavored to make women of the Yakima Valley more flight minded.

In 1930, after receiving her solo pilot's license, Maude traveled with the Pacific Northwest Air Tour. Forty planes started out on the tour of sixteen Northwest cities and towns. Maude's plane was one of the few that actually completed the circuit, making all of the sixteen scheduled stops. The Pacific Northwest Air Tour had great educational value for the visitors at local airports, as well as for the pilots. Maude claimed that participating had greatly increased her confidence in her solo flying skills.

The next year, in 1931, while enroute to an air meet in Cleveland, Ohio, Maude's plane was involved in a collision. She was one of four pilots traveling from Seattle to Cleveland as part of the Pacific Northwest Air Tour. Maude's plane was the first of the four to land. Minutes after landing her plane at an airstrip in Montana, it was hit by a Seattle plane attempting to land. The Seattle pilot had entered a crosscurrent of wind as he attempted his landing, causing it to collide with Maude's plane on the landing strip. Both planes were demolished; only the engine and propeller were salvaged from Maude's plane. She received some compensation from the other pilot and expected to be able to buy a new plane. Her husband, Charles Bolin, drove to Montana from their home in Toppenish to retrieve his wife.

While flying, problems Maude encountered included inclement weather, poor visibility, and overheating radiators—all inherent dangers to a solo Northwest pilot. On another occasion Maude's biplane struck a tractor during a landing, shearing off a wing.

Flying airplanes was just Maude's latest venture in feminine independence. Her earlier career as a cowgirl and rodeo performer also required a great deal of courage, skill, and endurance. Maude performed with the Spain Brothers' rodeo shows throughout the West. A daredevil, she often raced horses in rodeos such as the Pendleton Round-Up, Ellensburg Rodeo, and Toppenish Pow Wow.

She frequently competed in the women's relay race, a top feature in Northwest rodeos. In the relays, one person holds the string of tough-mouthed, relay ponies, while the rider makes the quick change of mount needed for the race. Riders were to run three laps on three different mounts, changing horses after each lap. The races were treacherous, requiring bravery and expert riding skills. Well into her thirties, Maude still rode in the relays during the Toppenish Pow Wow, although she admitted that participating in the contest without practice was now difficult.

MAUDE C. LILLIE BOLIN

* * *

Maude's roots were in the Northwest's earliest pioneer days. Her father was the first white settler on the Yakama* Indian Reservation, in the Yakima Valley. Her mother was a member of the Yakama Indian Tribal Nation, as was Maude. The Yakama Reservation was created by treaty in 1855, which was ratified by Congress in 1858. White men were not allowed to enter the reservation without the tribe's permission and the approval of the Indian Agency.

Nevada Lillie, Maude's father, had crossed the plains to settle in the Washington Territory. He drove stagecoaches throughout central Washington. Nevada was a pioneer with a large interest of livestock. He contributed substantially to the development of the Yakima Valley. In addition to ranching and driving stage, Nevada served for many years as a United States deputy marshall. Josephine (Bowzer) Lillie, Maude's mother, earned the title as, "Mother of Toppenish," because forty of her eighty acres of Indian allotment land was platted to become the business district for the town of Toppenish.

Congress passed the Allotment Act of 1887 with the idea of turning Indians into farmers by allotting them from 40 to 160 acres of land in their own names instead of the tribe's. The 1912 census showed 4,548 allotments had been issued to Yakama tribal members, with each man, woman, and child receiving a typical tract of eighty acres. Unlike reservation land, the allotments (with the granting of a fee patent approved by the Department of Indian Affairs) could become deeded land vested in the owner's name and sold to white settlers. The results of the act were sometimes disastrous, as individual Indians who were uninterested in farming, sold or lost their land to taxes. By the time the act was repealed fifty years later,

---

*Recently the Yakama Tribe resumed the traditional spelling of their name, rather than using "Yakima" as the city and valley do.

Indian land holdings in the United States had dropped from 136 million acres to only fifty million acres.

No one took advantage of Josephine Lillie, a progressive, forward-looking woman, vitally interested in community affairs. Josie filed her plat with the Yakima County Commission on April 4, 1905. The platted land became the business district of Toppenish. Toppenish is the Yakama term for "sloping and spreading" and describes the sloping plains of the west end of the reservation's valley. The town boomed, and lots within the forty acres sold like "hotcakes." This became the first deeded land on the Yakama Reservation.

A trading post license was granted to the Lillies by the government in 1890. They erected a small building and opened a store and post office. Josephine served as the town's postmistress and operated the first store. Maude Claire Lillie, born on July 25, 1891, was the fifth of eight children born to the Lillies.

Nevada and Josie Lillie separated in 1898, and Josephine, seeking a better education for her children, moved them to Portland, Oregon. Maude studied drama, elocution, and millinery at the Western Academy of Elocution and Dramatics. In a 1929 newspaper interview, Maude stated her original goals,

> I wanted to be an actress always, but though I studied for a career on the stage my mother would never give her sanction to such "wild" plans. I served six months' apprentice as a beauty parlor worker once and again I learned the millinery trade by serving a six months' apprenticeship there.

On August 1, 1911, Maude Claire Lillie married Charles F. Bolin, a prominent attorney, cowboy, and Yakima Valley baseball star. The Bolins built a grand manor in Toppenish, the finest home located on the Yakama Indian Reservation. Their mansion was centered on an eighty-acre ranch comprised of Maude's allotment, adjoining the town of Toppenish. Although the couple had no children of their own, for a time they raised two children belonging to Maude's sister.

Maude became an experienced rodeo performer and ran her own round-up business in Toppenish. At their ranch, Maude and Charley Bolin organized the first Indian Fair and Round Up in Toppenish, later taking their show on the road. In these shows, Maude performed with many notable rodeo cowboys and cowgirls of the day. Maude's Yakama Indian ancestors were known as accomplished horse riders. When Lewis and Clark explored the Northwest in 1805, the Yakamas had been horsemen for seventy-five years.

Her career as a professional rodeo rider began with the Spain Brothers' Western Show. John Spain, the handsome gentleman cowboy, was a renown bronc rider in his day. As a young man, John won the title in the World Championship Saddle Broncbusting Contest at the second Pendleton Round-Up, held in 1911. In the famous incident, after a last-go-around, one judge's vote settled a three-way-tie between John, George Fletcher (the famous black cowboy), and Jackson Sundown (a noted Nez Perce bronc rider). John continued to win rodeo purses even after losing his hand in a roping accident.

Maude, a pretty, dark-eyed brunette, was also a sought-after singer who was often featured at important Toppenish weddings, funerals, and social affairs. The talented lady might one day be found daintily pouring tea at a social affair, and the next day be seen clad in soiled coveralls at the airport.

Using her dramatic and musical training, Maude directed young members of her tribe in a gala production of *Hiawatha's Wedding Feast*, performed for the community in 1936. It was the first time a Northwest production had used Indian actors and actresses exclusively in a production about Indians. Maude took great satisfaction in helping the Yakama actors, mostly high-school students or younger, achieve success with the production. She was proud of the youngsters, feeling many of them had voices that with training would far surpass the ordinary. Maude reported,

> There was not a trained voice among them. As for the dances—well, of course, they did not need training for them. They were dances every Indian child knows from the time he can stand and walk and run. They didn't rehearse those—they just did them. The dances were outstanding features to the pageant.

To make the most of the limited time permitted for practice before the performance, Maude said she repeatedly summoned to their minds the stately memory of their grandparents, and they responded by fitting their actions to that memory.

Maude again directed young Yakamas in a presentation of *Sacajawea*, performed at the 1948 Toppenish Pow Wow. *Sacajawea*, had a cast of 120 people, mostly tribal members. The pageant was performed on three successive nights at the Toppenish Pow Wow and was host to most of the population of the Yakima Valley. Maude's goal was to put on a show using young Native American performers that was historically accurate as well as emotionally appealing. This endeavor was a great success.

An asset to her community, Maude was called upon to lead a wide variety of community projects. In 1942, she headed the local United China Relief Committee which succeeded in raising more than the Toppenish quota of contributions for Chinese war relief during World War II. She appealed to the citizens of Toppenish stating, "Contributions will help to maintain Chinese moral at this supreme hour of crisis and keep open our one unbroken fighting front in the Far East."

In 1946, the town of Toppenish sponsored a drive to have its own general hospital. Maude generously contributed three quarters of an acre of land for the site of the Central Memorial Hospital, now known as Providence Hospital, which opened its doors in 1951.

In 1950, Maude, with the assistance of the city of Toppenish and the Chamber of Commerce, appealed to the Commissioner of Indian Affairs in Washington, D.C., for a fee patent on her allotted land in order to deed it over to the city of Toppenish. The allotted land was held in trust for Maude as a member of the Yakama Tribe and could not be deeded to a non-Indian without permission of the Department of Indian Affairs. The trust land lay across several streets within city limits, and the land was needed to extend the city limits and ensure the continued growth of the town of Toppenish. The patent was approved, and Maude's land was annexed to the city, becoming "Bolin's Green Addition."

Another act of Maude's generosity was to offer to donate her home to the town of Toppenish as a museum for the purpose of preserving antiques, historical relics, and art of both the Yakama people and the settlers. The gracious Bolin mansion, built in 1911, shortly after Maude's marriage to Charles Bolin, was a focal point in Toppenish. Mrs. Bolin stated, "I want to donate my home as a memorial to my mother, the mother of Toppenish. All of the wonderful handcrafts and arts of the Indians and the history of this reservation town should be preserved for posterity." Unfortunately, the city, fearing a lack of funds would prevent them from maintaining the home, refused the offer. The city did accept Maude's donation of land for a city park. The park was named Pioneer Park and dedicated to the memory of local pioneers.

In 1959, she was sent as a local representative from Region V to a White House Conference on Children and Youth. The Toppenish Pow Wow named July 2, 1960, Maude Bolin Day, in honor of all that she had contributed to the Pow Wow and to her town. Maude passed away just six years later, on February 17, 1966, at the age of seventy-four.

Professional cowgirl, singer, aviator, drama coach, community leader—all of this comprised the multifaceted character of Maude Bolin. As a role model for the community and for her Yakama Tribe, Maude modeled independence, courage, and diversity at a time when women were expected to find fulfillment solely in the home. ❖

PANG YEE CHING

1892–1992

Journey to "Gam Saan"

*B*ags packed, ready to disembark, the young Chinese bride listened to the hustle and bustle of the passengers on the upper decks shuffling their luggage about as they prepared to leave the ship. The ship, US *Mongolia*, was now docked in San Francisco Bay, and the first- and second-class passengers were disembarking. Soon, thought Yee Ching, her family would be free to enter *"Gam Saan,"* the golden hills of America, to pursue their dream of building a new life.

Yee Ching, five months pregnant with her first child, had already endured nearly two months of difficult ocean travel in the ship's crowded, lowest-class quarters. Not only had she been confined to the underbelly of the ship during most of the voyage, but she and her husband had been housed next to the boiler room throughout the trip. Now, the journey had ended; she could not wait to begin life in America with her husband of just one year.

Yee Ching and her husband, Lee Je Yuen, found their excitement to be short lived. The couple now had to wait in what seemed an endless line for their papers to be inspected by U.S. immigration officials. "Do not worry," Je Yuen assured his young wife, "Our

Pang Yee Ching

papers are in order, there will be no problem." What was happening? The Lees watched as some well-dressed Chinese people were directed off the ship, but others were sent toward a smaller boat waiting on the pier.

Finally, an immigration official examined their papers and asked Je Yuen questions which he answered in broken English. When the official had finished questioning the couple, the official pointed to the waiting boat, "That way." Confused and frightened, the couple followed directions. The Lees now found themselves aboard a small boat bound for an isolated island in San Francisco Bay where they were told there would be more questions. The Lees, like most Chinese immigrants from 1910 to 1940, were being sent to Angel Island to face an intimidating immigration process.

When they arrived at Angel Island,* Yee Ching felt her heart drop as she was directed to a building on one side of the camp, and her husband to another. She was led to a long barracks which contained about one hundred metal-framed beds with dingy bedding. Guards locked the doors to the barracks behind her. Yee Ching was separated from her husband for the next few weeks; she was assigned a number, fed boiled meat and vegetables which often made her and the others sick, and subjected to humiliating physical examinations and terrifying interrogations.

The interrogations consisted of a series of mundane, irrelevant questions about the immigrants themselves, their families, and their villages in China. If the interrogators detected any inconsistencies in the immigrants' answers, they were sent back to their barracks to await further questioning on another day. Many Chinese immigrants failed to satisfy the interrogators due to their fear and nervousness at being grilled and confined in such a manner.

The Chinese Exclusion Act, prohibiting Chinese laborers from

---

*The description of the Lee's stay on Angel Island is based on a compilation of Chinese immigrants' experiences, rather than on specific memories described by Yee Ching.

immigrating and denying citizenship to newly arrived Chinese, was passed in 1882. Merchants, teachers, students, and visitors were exempt from this law but still could not become U.S. citizens. The Angel Island Immigration Compound was built to enforce the Chinese Exclusion Act. For the first time in American history, a group of people were denied entry into the country based solely on their race. The Chinese Exclusion Act was not repealed until 1943. Some Chinese were detained for months, or even years. The Lees were quarantined on Angel Island for two weeks before being allowed to enter the country.

* * *

The third of seven children, Pang Yee Ching was born to Pang Shu Kaui and Chung Chow Ying on December 30, 1892, in Fa Yuen, Gow Yuen Chong Village in Canton, China. The Gow Yuen Chong Village in Fa Yuen, Canton, was populated by 100 people, all members of the Pang family, who spoke the *"Hack Ga"* dialect. Most in the village were hard-working farmers who grew vegetables, sugar cane, sweet potatoes, and taro root. Extended families lived under the same roof where grandparents cared for the children while both mothers and fathers worked in the fields. The village centered around a large pond in which fish were raised both to feed the villagers and for market.

At age three, Yee Ching moved with her family to Hong Kong. Her father, Pang Shu Kuai, had worked as a jade cutter in his native village, but in hope of a brighter future, he moved his family to Hong Kong where he took a job as a custodian and messenger for the American Wellesley Presbyterian Church. As part of his compensation, the family was provided living quarters at the rear of the church. Though cramped, these accommodations were modern by comparison to their windowless, tile-roofed village home constructed of bricks mixed with clay, mud, rice, and wheat. In Hong Kong his children were educated by the Presbyterian missionaries. It was here that Pang Shu Kuai and his family converted from Buddhism to Christianity.

Even though it was unusual for Chinese families to educate their daughters, Yee Ching and her older sister, Tai Yee, were sent to boarding school in Canton. At eleven years of age, Yee Ching and her sister set out on a three-day boat trip before arriving at the Sok Ching Elementary School in Canton. The family paid one dollar per month for tuition, room, and board for each student.

After six years of study at Sok Ching, Yee Ching, an exemplary student, was asked by the school's principal to teach school. The principal secured special permission from Yee Ching's parents and then hired the sixteen-year-old to teach grades one through three. She sent for her younger sister, Yee Paw, and supported her on a meager teaching salary. At first, Yee Ching found teaching school difficult because of her young age and lack of teaching experience. Many days she was reduced to tears of frustration. Still, she continued teaching at Sok Ching for three more years.

While teaching in the Hoy San District, Yee Ching met her husband, Lee Je Yuen. Lee Je Yuen had graduated from the Presbyterian Theological Seminary in Canton, China, on January 12, 1911. At that time in China, arranged marriages were the norm, but Yee Ching and Je Yuen fell in love. Observing tradition, Yee Ching's father took *"Hom Toy,"* or salted greens, to the Lee family village as a gift prior to the wedding.

Pang Yee Ching and Lee Je Yuen were married in a Presbyterian church in Canton on January 1, 1914. Yee Ching wore a light blue silk dress and a white veil. She and her bridesmaid were carried to the church in a traditional bridal chair shouldered by two attendants.

After her marriage, Yee Ching continued to teach while Je Yuen attended school in Canton to learn English. The couple dreamed of coming to America. Je Yuen applied to the American Consulate in Hong Kong for the papers needed to go to America. In addition, he took a test to ensure he had the proper qualifications to teach in the United States. Using borrowed money for their passage, the young couple boarded the US *Mongolia* for America in 1915.

Following their two-week detention on Angel Island, the Lees settled in Los Angeles's Chinatown where they were hired to teach Chinese to Chinatown's young residents. The school was adjacent to a church, and the Lees were given living quarters in half of the school building. They later moved into Je Yuen's brother's home. Both Yee Ching and her husband became ill with tuberculosis during their first few years in Los Angeles. Yee Ching was sent to a sanitarium for recovery.

When his friend, Lee Yick Soo, retired as minister of Los Angeles's Chinese Presbyterian Church, Je Yuen was called upon to be the church's pastor. An integral part of the church, Yee Ching taught Sunday school, worked with the Women's Association, and was the church pianist. Yee Ching had learned to play the organ at the school in China simply by watching the organist. She not only played the old piano at the back of the church for her family as a girl, but taught her younger siblings to play.

Both Yee Ching and Je Yuen continued their work as teachers at the Chinese school. During this ten-year period, the couple was blessed with three children, whom they taught to speak their father's native Hoy San dialect. The children also attended classes at the church school where their parents taught.

After his contract with the church expired in 1925, Je Yuen decided to return to China to continue his ministry. He proceeded to apply for passage to China for his entire family. With China in the throes of constant political and economic turmoil, Yee Ching vehemently opposed returning the family to their native land. Her staunch argument was that, not only was the timing bad, but they could not ignore the fact that America offered far superior, unlimited educational opportunities for the growth of their children. In a surprising display of independence for a Chinese wife, she told her husband that if he returned to China, she would not go with him.

While all of this was being considered, a family friend, Tom Foo Yuen, convinced Je Yuen to move with him to Spokane, Washington, to run an herb shop he had purchased. The pregnant Yee Ching and her children moved in with a cousin while her husband traveled to Washington to start the business. That fall of 1926, Yee Ching gave birth to her fourth child.

When her husband sent for her in 1927, Yee Ching and her four children traveled three days by train to a new, unknown western city, Spokane. Tom Foo Yuen and Lee Je Yuen formed a partnership and named their business Foo Yuen Herb Company. Tom taught Je Yuen and Yee Ching the herbal profession. For five thousand years, Chinese herbalists have passed on the art of herb gathering and healing from generation to generation. The partners hired a Chinese herb pharmacist to help with the business, but within two years of the shop's inception, the hired pharmacist left the company, and Mr. Tom retired. This left Yee Ching as her husband's sole professional assistant in his business. The children helped out with the business, performing clerical and custodial duties at early ages, just as Yee Ching had helped her family earn their living in China.

Due to the Lee family's hard work, the business endured although the herb shop's first years of operation were slow. Yee Ching's innovations aided in the business' eventual prosperity. The Foo Yuen Herb Company was located over the Manning Cafe in downtown Spokane. When she heard the cafe's proprietors talking about obtaining new kitchen appliances, Yee Ching marched into the restaurant and asked them what they were planning to do with their old electric coffee grinder. Surprised, the proprietors presented Yee Ching with the grinder for a small fee. The Lees were then able to grind their precious imported Chinese herbs more efficiently and with less effort than the old mortar and pestle had required.

The Foo Yuen Herb Company sold nothing but Chinese herbs, gathered wild in the mountains of China. During World War II, importing became difficult and exorbitantly expensive. Fortunately, the Lees had had the foresight to stockpile Chinese herbs before the war began and had enough herbs saved to avoid the high prices of importing during the war years. Without these efforts, the Foo Yuen Herb Company might not have survived World War II.

Upon entering the herb shop, customers were greeted by a tangy, pungent, spicy aroma. Glass cases contained a variety of barks, roots, leaves, and shoots waiting to be ground, steeped, and used as remedies for rheumatism, nervous disorders, weakness, stomach pains, colds, and flu. Patients often sought out the Lees for treatment as a last resort for curing their ails. Most of their customers were Caucasians, rather than Chinese, and more European immigrants than Americans sought treatment. Germans especially believed in the Chinese herbal treatments.

In addition to riding the cable cars into downtown Spokane to work at the herb company, Yee Ching raised her seven children in their humble wood and coal-heated home. She grew her own vegetables and herbs, as proper Chinese vegetables could not be found in Spokane. Using her clothesline, Yee Ching hung bunches of greens out to dry and made traditional "*hom toy*," or salted greens. In the hot summer, she canned fruits and jams over her wood-fueled range. Her "Maytag" washing machine was a blessing compared to the hand-carved bamboo washboards she had used in China. Even with this modern convenience, she rinsed her laundry in the upstairs bathtub in order to preserve the soapy water for multiple loads of wash.

The Lees purchased their first home in America in Spokane near St. Luke's Hospital. The location of their house proved useful, as Yee Ching walked to the hospital for the delivery of her next three babies, twin boys and a girl. Even with the addition of a third bedroom, which Yee Ching had insisted her husband have built, the family—now with seven children—was crowded in their small home. During her early years in China, Yee Ching had been raised in a small dirt-floored house that had been home to her family for generations. Many family members shared the home with each other, as well as with village chickens, pigs, and cows. When thinking back to her childhood, this small house in Spokane, though crowded, must have seemed very modern with its running water and indoor bathroom.

There were very few Chinese people in Spokane in the early Twentieth century. At one time, the Chinese community in and around Spokane had been much larger. A *Spokesman-Review* reporter estimated the Chinese population in 1888 at approximately six hundred. These were mostly young men brought over in the 1860s to build the railroads. Prior to that, Chinese prospectors mined for gold with dreams of making a fortune and returning to China. It was not legal for any of these workers to bring wives into the United States. Only American-born Chinese, Chinese dignitaries, and a few merchants were allowed to do so. By the 1940s, Spokane's Chinese population had dwindled to approximately one hundred. As a result, for the first four decades of this century, there were very few Chinese women in Spokane and Yee Ching had little female companionship. This was in sharp contrast to her Los Angeles days, when she worked in the Chinese church surrounded by many lady members and friends.

Although Yee Ching missed this aspect of her life, the dual role she now had of being a working mother did not leave her much leisure time. She pushed aside thoughts of loneliness and concentrated on her priority of being a good mother, centering her leisure moments around her children. She homeschooled the four youngest children in Chinese, teaching them the fundamentals of reading and writing, along with Chinese prayers, songs and rhymes. They, in turn, helped her gain proficiency reading English.

Through her creativity and resourcefulness, Yee Ching enhanced their playtimes too. She helped her children make newspaper kites; race cars from empty thread spools, wax, and rubber bands; wooden guns with strips of old inner tubes for ammunition; slingshots from tree branches; and wooden scooters with cast-off roller skate wheels. She genuinely enjoyed playing along with her children. In her later years, she played mahjong and American and Chinese checkers with her friends and family, but she also enjoyed more active endeavors. She relished the games of pool, ping-pong, and hitting golf and tennis balls. At age eighty-eight, Yee Ching fell and broke her hip while playing badminton!

The Foo Yuen Herb Company operated in Spokane from 1925 to 1957, when the Lees retired and returned to Hong Kong for a visit while their new house was being built in Spokane. Mr. Lee died in 1971, following complications from a stroke. His obituary lauded Lee Je Yuen as a revered leader in Spokane's Chinese community. Je Yuen was head of the *Kuo Min Tang*, a Chinese political organization founded by Generalissimo Chiang K'ai-shek. The *Tang* (not to be confused with a *Tong*, or Chinese secret society) was the main avenue for money sent to buy supplies for the Chinese Army to defend China against the invading Japanese Army during World War II. The Lees were responsible for supervising Spokane's collections for Chinese war relief. Like other Chinese-Americans, the Lees were required to wear buttons identifying them as Chinese, rather than Japanese, during World War II.

Je Yuen and Yee Ching held church services in their home, with Yee Ching playing the piano and directing hymn singing. In her later years, Mrs. Lee was often called upon to say eulogies for deceased members of the Chinese community, whether she knew them or not.

When invited to participate in planning a formal Chinese church in Spokane, Yee Ching, then a widow, enthusiastically agreed. She opened up her home for meetings and worship services. Finally, the Chinese Baptist Church of Spokane was established in the early 1970s. The Chinese community in Spokane had grown considerably by this time and church attendance was promising. Yee Ching was very proud to be a founding member of the church. Until her death, she was a loyal supporter of the church and enjoyed involvement in all of its activities. Once again, she had found a home in a Chinese church and the fellowship and camaraderie she had been deprived of in her early years of living in eastern Washington.

A long anticipated visit occurred when Yee Paw, Yee Ching's sister, arrived for a visit from Hong Kong. Yee Paw, or Fifth Auntie as the children called her, was the sister Yee Ching had supported in Hong Kong with her small teaching salary. Both sisters, now well into their eighties, were hard of hearing, so they communicated by writing notes to each other in Chinese. Yee Ching, eighty-four, took her younger sister rowing on Hayden Lake, and the two enjoyed many mahjong games together before Yee Paw returned to Hong Kong.

Yee Ching's eldest daughter, a retired public school teacher, began tutoring several Chinese immigrants from Hong Kong and Taiwan who were eager to learn English. They met in the daughter's home, gathering around the breakfast nook. Yee Ching, who was living with her daughter, was then in her eighties. Whenever students came, Yee Ching joined in the class with enthusiasm! Her interest was twofold; not only did she relish the opportunity to improve her own English, but she knew she could help in teaching. When her daughter could not get an explanation across to her students in either Cantonese or fumbling Mandarin, Yee Ching would bridge the gap and write in Chinese characters, since the written characters are exactly the same, irrespective of spoken dialects. Indeed, she still had the knack of teaching!

Though she raised her children in a mostly Caucasian community, with no support system and little English, Lee Yee Ching's seven children were all exceptional students who went on to become class officers and valedictorians. Three of Yee Ching's sons became doctors, one became a dentist, and the fourth son and two daughters became educators.

When one of her daughters agonized over the decision to marry a Caucasian, Yee Ching strongly and convincingly encouraged her, showing a wisdom and tolerance uncommon for older Chinese in the early 1950s. As she often told her children, "We are all made out of the same dough, when God put us in the oven to bake, some just came out a little browner, and with different features." Yee Ching was right, America—"*Gam Saan*"—did offer her children golden opportunities. She and her husband were very proud of their children's educational achievements, their military and professional careers, and their subsequent marriages and families.

Yee Ching Lee died on December 31, 1992, one day after her one hundredth birthday. A teacher, pastor's wife, business owner, founding member of Spokane's Chinese Baptist Church, mother, grandmother, and great-grandmother—Yee Ching Lee had been an inspiration to those who knew her throughout her one hundred years. ✚

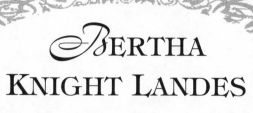

ℬERTHA KNIGHT LANDES
1868–1943

Mayor of Seattle

*W*inking at the city council president who would be acting mayor in his absence, Mayor Brown instructed her to "keep an eye on the chief of police." Seattle Mayor, Edwin ("Doc") J. Brown, was getting ready to leave town and travel east to the 1924 Democratic National Convention in New York City. Doc Brown, a dentist, had been a tolerance mayor, allowing his chief of police to run the city with a free hand. Gambling, graft, and prostitution flourished during his administration. In contrast, the highly pricipled president of the city council, Bertha Knight Landes, was a blue-nosed, strong-willed, reform administrator who had been encouraged into civic life by members of the many women's clubs over which she had presided.

As soon as Doc Brown's train was headed east, Mrs. Landes took it upon herself to move her office down the hall from the city council chambers into the mayor's executive suite in the County-City Building. Before moving, she aired the executive office thoroughly, as Doc Brown was a heavy cigar smoker.

Her next act was to charge the Police Department with corruption. Mrs. Landes wrote to the Chief of Police William B.

MUSEUM OF HISTORY AND INDUSTRY

Bertha Knight Landes

Severyns stating, "The Police Department has lost the confidence of the people. The innocent men are under the stigma of graft, bootlegging and connivance with crime, as well as the guilty."

She gave Severyns twenty-four hours to do something about the open liquor sales (then illegal), gambling, and vice that was rampant throughout the city.

In an attempt to pacify the acting mayor, Severyns admitted that "about 100 policemen ought to be fired." Bertha then pronounced, in a well-publicized ultimatum, that the chief was to fire the one hundred men or be dismissed himself. Chief Severyns replied smugly, "Well, why don't you do it yourself!" That was all she needed! Bertha Landes issued her General Order Number I and assumed control of the Seattle Police Department. She delegated her powers to Ballard Police Captain, Claude Bannick. Bannick had been chief of police during an earlier reform-minded administration and possessed an impeccable reputation for honesty.

The two announced their intentions to dismiss two civil service commissioners and one hundred members of the police department. They proceeded to raid and close down bars, pool and gambling halls, honky-tonks, and speakeasies all over Seattle.

Doc Brown's people at city hall were beside themselves but powerless to stop the acting mayor. They wired Brown to get back to Seattle on the first train west and hatched a scheme to quell Mrs. Landes's enthusiasm for reform.

Brown's secretary, Henry J. Dahlby, sneaked into the mayoral suite before the office opened and put two suitcases on the floor by Mayor Brown's desk. Next, he placed Doc Brown's hat atop the desk, filled the office with cigar smoke, and left a cigar butt in the ashtray. A press release was issued, allegedly by Brown, that he had "no comment to make on the current situation" with the city government.

Whether or not Bertha Landes fell for this act is subject to interpretation. Things did calm down until Mayor Brown's train arrived a day or so after the ruse had been executed. He, of course, immediately rescinded all of acting Mayor Landes's reforms.

This incident may have paved the way for a grand jury investigation and movement in favor of Doc Brown's impeachment.* Bertha Knight Landes ran for mayor of Seattle in 1926 on a platform against sin and vice and in favor of municipal government restructuring. "Rectitude in government, civic decency, and public morality!" was her campaign cry.

Seattle, long known for some of the most corrupt municipal officials in the nation, was ready for a "woman's touch." To Bertha, city government was "but a larger housekeeping."

---

*A King County Grand Jury investigated and ultimately criticized Brown's administration but did not find enough evidence to indict or impeach him; they decided to let the voters decide his fate.

* * *

She was born Bertha Ethel Knight on October 19, 1868, in Ware, Massachusetts, a town west of Boston. Bertha was the youngest of nine children born to Charles Sanford Knight and Cordelia (Cutter) Knight. Charles Knight worked as a painter and real estate agent but was later incapacitated by time-aggravated wounds he had suffered during the Civil War.

In 1891, Bertha Knight graduated with a degree in history from Indiana University, where her sister's husband was the college president. Moving home with her mother, she taught school for three years before becoming engaged to Henry Landes, a geology student obtaining his graduate degree from Harvard. The two were married on January 2, 1894. A year later, Henry was appointed professor of geology at the University of Washington.

The couple arrived in Seattle in 1895 to a new University of Washington campus. The campus had recently moved from its former downtown Seattle location to one north of Seattle where it is presently located. Their home, where they would live for twenty years, was built on Brooklyn and Forty-fifth Street, where Meany Tower now stands. Very much the faculty wife, Bertha entertained frequently and raised two children as her husband rose to the position of dean of the College of Sciences.

Three children were born to the Landeses: two sons and a daughter. Katherine, the eldest, died at the age of nine of complications resulting from a tonsillectomy. Roger died as an infant. Only Kenneth lived to adulthood, becoming a professor of geology at the University of Michigan. Two years after Katherine's death, Bertha and Henry adopted a nine-year-old daughter, Viola. Bertha also cared for a blind, elderly uncle for some time.

As her children grew older, Bertha became more and more involved in community service groups and women's clubs. Always rising to the top, Bertha served as president of the Congregational Church Women's League, the League of Women Voters, Red Cross Auxiliary, Women's University Club, and Seattle Federation of Women's Clubs. Working in these organizations, Bertha honed her public speaking skills and familiarity with democratic procedure.

As president of the Seattle Federation of Women's Clubs, she was responsible for putting on a weeklong Women's Education Exhibit for Washington manufacturers. Seattle's business community was so impressed with her work that she was lauded by the Seattle Chamber of Commerce and appointed, by the mayor, as the only woman on a five-member commission to study unemployment in the city.

Her success on the commission inspired a fellow member to urge Bertha to run for city council. Bertha Landes had jumped from traditional women's church and community clubs into the world of business, politics, and civic service. She believed that women should raise their families before entering politics and not be dependent on their salary for income; however, even women with small children at home should be attentive to the outside world. Although she still advocated home and family as a woman's first responsibility, during her 1922 campaign, Bertha stated that the time had come for women to be represented in city government. "It is not only the right, but the privilege and duty, of women to take part in the administration of public affairs."

The campaign for city council was run by five of her fellow club members, all housewives with no previous political experience. The group ran a low-budget campaign without "slush funds"—no paid campaign workers, promised jobs, or obligations to contributors. Her supporters thought it was important for Bertha to enter office "with clean hands," not owing favors to anyone. Henry Landes was his wife's staunchest supporter. This was not a stretch for Henry, long known for his support of women students and faculty at the

University of Washington. Both of the Landeses saw public office as a civic duty, not a furtherance of one's own political ambition.

On May 22, 1922, Bertha Knight Landes and Kathryn Miracle were elected to the city council, breaking through an all-male barricade into city government. Bertha was elected by a record margin of 22,000 votes. On the day of her election, Councilman Landes talked to reporters.

Our campaign is over. It has been strictly a women's campaign to elect a woman to the city council without entangling alliances, to represent women's thoughts and viewpoints. . . . Our idea was to serve the best interests of the city; not to further the political ambitions of any one woman.

In fact, fifty-eight-year-old Bertha Landes was quite reluctant to run for mayor in 1926. She changed her mind many times and only filed to run on the last possible day. Bertha eventually decided to run because she believed that she was the only candidate that had a chance of ousting Doc Brown.

Winning by a margin of six thousand votes, Bertha Knight Landes set a new Seattle electoral record and became the first woman mayor of a major city in America. She did not believe that politics had any place in city government and could not be influenced as those who preceded her had been. Bertha's administration was honest and scandal free. The new mayor reorganized city government and cleaned up the streets of Seattle. Qualified professionals were appointed to head city departments. The City Light Department and the Board of Public Works were completely revamped. Seattle's financial mess was ironed out, stricter law enforcement was stressed, the Park Department and recreational programs were expanded, and the rail car system was improved for travel on city streets. One of the first to do so, she advocated a merger between city and county governments.

Insisting on full equality, she disdained the title of councilwoman or mayoress, preferring to be addressed as councilman and mayor. She explained, "Let women who go into politics be the real thing or nothing! Let us, while never forgetting our womanhood, refrain from all emphasis on sex and put it on being public servants."

Bertha enjoyed official ceremonies and was often photographed at groundbreakings, in parades, and with celebrities visiting town, including Will Rogers, Queen Marie of Romania, and Charles Lindberg. She was quoted in the *Seattle Post-Intelligencer* on October 30, 1927, as saying, "Frankly, I like being Mayor. I haven't seen any reason, since taking office, why a woman can't fill it as well as a man."

As the nation's only major metropolitan woman mayor, she received a great deal of publicity. *The New York Times* and *Sunset Magazine* wrote of her "simple attitude, gentle manner and great poise." She was backed by the national press, women's clubs, and many businessmen. Bertha encouraged more women to seek public office and spoke of government as a "joint man and woman affair."

This national notoriety also worked against Mayor Landes. Were Seattle men "sissies?" Easterners inquired. Taunts like "the great open space, where men are men and women are mayors" became common. Some local businessmen felt such comments were damaging their images and would hurt business with other cities. Bertha had also made enemies with her liquor raids and stringent reforms. Believing in public utilities, she had clashed with private power companies over both the railcar system and Seattle City Light. Restructuring government had also meant personnel cuts, which were not very popular with city employees.

In 1928, Frank Edwards ran against Mayor Landes on a platform of "No more petticoat government." Edwards was a complete political unknown, with absolutely no record of public service or civic involvement; however, his campaign was heavily financed by private interests. Bertha Knight Landes was defeated by 19,000 votes. Somewhat bitter about her defeat, but stoically and with good humor, she left office.

Still involved in community affairs, she remained active with a busy schedule of lecturing, travel, and continuing community service. In 1933, Dean Landes and Bertha led the first of four University study tours to Asia. Henry Landes became ill on the last trip, developing bronchitis from which he died in Seattle in 1936. As her last public act, Bertha led the next Asian tour alone.

In failing health, she moved to California in 1941, hoping for improvement with the climate. Bertha Knight Landes passed away six weeks after her seventy-fifth birthday, on November 29, 1943, at her son's home in Ann Arbor, Michigan.

The city of Seattle has never elected another woman mayor. Though she was only in office for two years, Bertha attempted efficient management of a major city; strengthened municipal utilities; sought to improve community services and programs; and enforced laws that she considered essential for the health and welfare of Seattle's citizens. By all measures, Bertha Landes was one of the most dedicated, efficient, and some think, the best mayor Seattle has ever known. ❧

BIBLIOGRAPHY

KICK-IS-OM-LO (PRINCESS ANGELINE)

"Angeline Is Non-committal." *The Seattle Press-Times*, 21 October 1891.

"Battle of Seattle." *The Seattle Press-Times*, 30 January 1892.

Conover, C. T. "Just Cogitating: Princess Angeline Was Familiar Figure in Seattle," *The Seattle Times*, 11 November 1956.

———. "Just Cogitating: Angeline Was Best-Known of Chief Seattle's Children." *The Seattle Times*, 15 December 1957.

———. "Just Cogitating: Angeline Wanted to Be Buried among Tillicums." *The Seattle Times*, 21 December 1958.

———. "Just Cogitating: Princess Angeline Was Noted Sight in Old Seattle." *The Seattle Times*, 19 July 1959.

Dorpat, Paul. "Princess Angeline's Shack." *The Seattle Times*, 13 May 1984.

Duncan, Don. "Gentle Reign of Angeline." Don Duncan's Driftwood Diary, *The Seattle Times*, 28 June 1970.

"Gift Recalls Local History." *Capitol Hill Times*, 17 September 1958.

"Chief Seattle and Angeline." *Kitsap County History*. Silverdale, Wash.: The Kitsap County Historical Society Book Committee, 1977.

"Poor Old Angeline, Only Living Child of the Great War Chief Seattle." *Seattle Post-Intelligencer*, 2 August 1891.

Princess Angeline—Obituary. *Seattle Post-Intelligencer*, 31 May 1896.

"'Princess Angeline' to Be Given Friday Afternoon in Frederick & Nelson Store Auditorium." *The Seattle Times*, 8 May 1930.

"A Princess Prophecies." *The Seattle Press-Times*, 31 March 1892.

Riley, Lori Jackson. "Grandmother and Princess Angeline." In *Incidents In the Life of a Pioneer Woman*. The State Association of The Daughters of the Pioneers of Washington, 1976.

"The Royal Family." *The Seattle Press-Times*, 7 April 1892.

Sayre, J. Willis. *This City of Ours*. Seattle, 1936.

"Seattle's Princess." *Seattle Mail & Herald*, 26 October 1901.

"She Was Very Ancient." *The Seattle Press-Times*, 21 October 1891.

ISABEL FRIEDLANDER ARCASA

Anderson, Eva. "Silico Saska Was Entiat's Indian." *Wenatchee World*, circa 1955.

Arcasa, Isabelle [*sic*] and Robert H. Ruby. "No Wrath Like That of an Indian Chief Scorned." *Columbia Magazine*, Fall 1987.

Barham, Melvin. "Isabel Arcasa Keeps Indian Heritage Alive." *Wenatchee World*, 23 November 1980.

Brown, John A. and Robert H. Ruby. "Isabel Arcasa, a Centennial Centenarian." *Columbia Magazine*, Fall 1989.

Connolly, Tom, S.J. Manuscript prepared from interview taped with Isabel Arcasa, 5 May 1979.

Connolly, Tom, S.J. "Stories about Isabel Arcasa." *Colville Tribal Tribune*, 1 December 1989.

Greene, Bernice. "Interview With Isabel Arcasa." 18 October 1977, 25 October 1977, Manuscripts from North Central Washington Museum collection, Wenatchee, WA.

Greene, Bernice. "The Oldest Colville Indian in the West! Isabel Arcasa Celebrates 100th Birthday." *Colville Tribal Tribune*, 1 December 1989.

Schmeltzer, Michael. "Our Pioneers Are Part of the Present." *Spokane Chronicle*, 26 May 1983.

Special Thanks to:
Maybelle and Sheila Gendron, daughter and granddaughter of Isabel Arcasa.

BIBLIOGRAPHY

Father Tom Connolly, S.J., of Sacred Heart Mission, DeSmet, Idaho.
Father Patrick Twohy, S.J., of Swinomish Spritual Centre, La Connor,
Washington.
Mark Behler, curator, North Central Washington Museum, Wenatchee,
Washington.
Jessica Sylvanus, Research Assistant, Okanogan County Historical Society,
Okanogan, Washington.

DR. NETTIE J. CRAIG ASBERRY

Andrews, Mildred Tanner. *Washington Women as Path Breakers.* Tacoma, Wash:
Junior League of Tacoma, 1989.

Bence, Erma. "Dr. Asberry, 96, Founder of NAACP Here, to be Honored
on Tuesday." *The Tacoma News Tribune,* 23 July 1961.

Bence, Erma. "Found—A Very Old Diploma." *The Tacoma News Tribune,*
2 October 1975.

7th Annual Catalogue Of The Kansas Conservatory Of Music, Kansas
State Historical Society Collection, Topeka, KS 1879.

Kellogg, Caroline. "Time Machine: Dr. Nettie Asberry: Music Fixed Her
Vision." *The Tacoma News Tribune,* 4 December 1977.

"May 11 Is Proclaimed Dr. Nettie Asberry Day." *The Tacoma News Tribune,*
1 May 1961.

"Nettie Asberry of NAACP Dies at 103." *The Tacoma News Tribune,*
18 November 1968.

Patterson, James H. "Tacoma NAACP Unit Is First in the West." *The Tacoma
News Tribune,* 14 February 1968.

"Tacoma Woman Dies at Age 103." *The Seattle Times,* 19 November 1968.

Meeting minutes and notes for The Federation Of Colored Women's
Organization, University Of Washington—Manuscripts Collection.

Whitney, Marci. "Harmony Between Races Was Music Teacher's Aim." *The
Tacoma News Tribune,* 18 April 1976.

MAUDE C. LILLIE BOLIN

Dietrich, Bill. "Washington Indians: Indian History Tells a Tale of Two Worlds—Struggle and Survival." *The Seattle Times*, 16 December 1985.

"Feminine Campaigner Uses Unusual Method." *The Yakima Daily Republic*, 22 July 1942.

"First Solo Air Flight." *Toppenish-Review*, 15 November 1929.

"Flying, Relay Riding, Music and Trade of Milliner are Mastered by Toppenish Woman as Life Pleasures." *The Yakima Daily Republic*, 4 October 1929.

"Four Have Close Call at Superior." *The Daily Missoulian*, 17 July 1931.

Foster, Ruth—Manuscripts from the files of The Toppenish Mural Society

"Freak Planes, Girl Pilots Intrigue Tex." *Spokane Chronicle*, 31 July 1930.

Haugen, Borg. "Pow Wow City Takes on Color with Banners and Cow boys." *Yakima Sunday Herald*, 20 June 1948.

An Illustrated History of Klickitat, Yakima & Kittitas Counties. Interstate Publishing Company, 1904.

"Indians Wearing Festival Regalia Present Play," *The Yakima Daily Republic*, 1936.

Mays, Theo. *100 Years—100 Women*. Yakima County: Yakima Valley Museum, 1989.

"Mrs. Bolin Undaunted by Recent Wreck in Montana," *The Yakima Daily Republic*, 22 July 1931.

Murphy, Joseph and Gilson Ross. Letters to Commissioner of Indian Affairs, 21 March 1950. Yakima Valley Museum Archives.

"Pow Wow Events Slated." *Yakima Sunday Herald*, 12 June 1960.

"Relief for China Drive Will Start." *Toppenish-Review*, 15 May 1942.

"Relief Fund Drive Nears $500 Goal." *Toppenish-Review*, 19 June 1942.

Rupp, Virgil. *Let 'R Buck: History of the Pendleton Round-Up*. Pendleton, Ore.: A Time for Growth, 1985.

BIBLIOGRAPHY

"Toppenish Focus of Agriculture." *Yakima Sunday Herald*, 1960.

"Toppenish Woman Tells of Stunt." *Yakima Republic*, 26 November 1928.

The Yakima Indian Reservation and the city of Toppenish. Pamphlet. Toppenish, Wash.:Toppenish Commercial Club, 1916.

Yakima Valley Museum files, clippings from unidentified newspapers:

> "Bolin Home May Be City Museum," circa 1960s.

> Haugen, Borg. "History Of Yakima Valley Washington," 1919.

> "Jeanette Wesley 16 Year Old as Sacajawea," 15 June 1948.

> "Maude Bolin in Airplane Crash," 18 July 1931.

> "Mrs. Bolin Back from Plane Tour," 19 August 1930.

> "Rodeo Invitation," circa 1960s.

> "Toppenish Plane Brings Home Honors from Pasco Annual Air Jubilee," 17 May 1930.

> "Woman Flies Cross Country," 31 August 31 1928.

Special Thanks to:

Lowell Evans, Toppenish Mural Society.
Martin Humphrey, Archivist/Librarian, Yakima Valley Museum.
Colleen Veomett, Librarian, Yakama Nations Library.
Virginia Tubbs, Umatilla County Historical Society, Pendleton, Oregon.

MARY ANN BOREN DENNY

Atkins, Frank R. "Schooner 'Exact' Brought Settlers to Alki Landing." Costello Scrapbook. Seattle Public Library.

Bagley, Clarence B. *Pioneer Seattle and Its Pioneers*. Seattle: Argus Press, 1928.

Beaver, Lowell J. *Historic Memories from Monuments and Plaques of Western Washington*. Trademark Historic Memories, 1960.

Buerge, David M. "Seattle's Pioneer Women." In *Washingtonians*. Seattle: Sasquatch Publishing, 1989.

Crowley, Veryle Morehouse. "The First Christmas at Alki Point." In *Incidents in the Life of a Pioneer Woman.* The State Association of The Daughters of the Pioneers of Washington, 1976.

Denny, Arthur. *Pioneer Days on Puget Sound.* Seattle: C.B. Bagley Printer, 1888/Seattle: The Alice Harriman Company, 1908.

"Dennys Celebrate: Its Wedding Day & Birthday Fete." *The Seattle Times,* 2 September 1933.

"Denny Family 'Stitch in Time' Is Historical." *The Seattle Times,* 11 December 1932.

Hanford, Cornelius. *Seattle and Environs.* Seattle: Pioneer Historical Publishing Co., 1924.

"Mrs. Arthur A. Denny Dead: Woman Founder of City Passes Away." *The Seattle Daily Times,* 30 December 1910.

Newell, Gordon. *Westward to Alki: The Story of David and Louisa Denny.* Seattle: Superior Publishing Company, 1977.

"Rolland Denny's Life of Integrity Spanned Era of City's Development." *Seattle Star,* 21 December 1947.

Sketches of Washingtonians. Seattle: Wellington C. Wolfe & Co., 1906.

A Volume of Memoirs and Genealogy of Representative Citizens of the City Of Seattle and King County Washington. New York and Chicago: The Lewis Publishing Company, 1903.

Watt, Roberta Frye. *Four Wagons West: The Story of Seattle.* Portland, Ore: Binford & Mort, 1931.

THEA CHRISTIANSEN FOSS

"City Makes It Official: Thea Foss Waterway." *The Morning News Tribune,* 18 October 1989.

Evans, Walter. "Thea Foss: Lasting Wake on Sound." *Seattle Post-Intelligencer,* 4 June 1976.

Foss, Andrew—Obituary. *The Seattle Times,* 14 March 1937.

BIBLIOGRAPHY

Foss, Henry. "A Mother Molds The Character of a Boy." *The Tacoma News Tribune*, 14 May 1967.

"From the Crow's Nest." *The Seattle Times*, 12 September 1935.

Green, Frank L. "Thea Foss—*A Gallery Of 100 Eminent Washingtonians.*" Tacoma, Wash.: Washington State Historical Society, 1989.

Johnson, Bruce and Michael Skalley. *Foss: a Living Legend.* Printed for Foss Maritime Company, 1990.

Michener, Charles T. "A Remarkable Saga of Tugs and Towing." *Seattle Magazine*, (1966): 39–43.

Skalley, Michael. "*Foss: Ninety Years Of Towboating.*" 23 August 1982.

"'Tugboat Annie' Continues Run." *Seattle Post-Intelligencer*, 4 August 1933.

"Tugboat Annie Picture to be Sold." *Seattle Post-Intelligencer*, 4 June 1976.

Whitney, Marci. "Thea Foss Was No 'Tugboat Annie.'" *The Tacoma News Tribune*, 19 September 1976.

Special Thanks to:

Kae Paterson, Commencement Bay Maritime Center.
Tim Brewer, Vice President, and Michael Skalley, Historian, Foss Maritime Company.

FAY FULLER

Duncan, Don. "With the First Woman atop Mount Rainier," Driftwood Diary. *The Seattle Times*, 14 January 1973.

Duncan, Don. "Climbers Commemorate Fuller's Rainier Ascent." *The Seattle Times*, 9 August 1990.

"Fay Fuller Reaches Top of Rainier." *The Tacoma News Tribune*, 10 August 1890. Reprint, 1 July 1976.

"Female Mountaineers' Clothes Streamlined." *The Tacoma News Tribune*, 11 July 1943.

"First Woman to Climb Rainier Liked Annual." *The Tacoma News Tribune*, 12 March 1950.

"First Woman to Conquer Mountain Dies." *The Tacoma News Tribune*, 27 May 1958.

Fuller, Fay. "A Trip to the Summit." *Every Sunday*, 23 August 1890.

Hunt, Katharine. "First Woman to Climb the Mountain Visits City." *The Tacoma News Tribune*, 17 August 1950.

Kellogg, Caroline. "Time Machine: Bloomer-Clad Fay Fuller's Trek Shocked Tacoma." *The Tacoma News Tribune*, 7 March 1982.

Linsley, Jeann. "Women Commemorate Fuller's Historic Ascent." *The Seattle Times*, 10 August 1990.

McIntyre, Bob. Transcript Of Interview with Mrs. Fritz Von Briesen, August 18, 1950, Mount Rainier National Park Service.

Molenaar, Dee. *The Challenge Of Rainier.* Seattle: The Mountaineers, 1971.

Potts, Betsey. "Fay Fuller—First Woman to the Top of Mount Rainier." *Columbia Magazine* 10 (Winter 1996-1997): 24–29.

Schullery, Paul. "Island in the Sky: Pioneering Accounts of Mount Rainier 1833-1894." Seattle: The Mountaineers, 1987.

Smith, Ernest C.. "A Trip to Mount Rainier," read April 11, 1898, Manuscript from the files of Mount Rainier National Park Service.

"Summit Salute to First Woman to Climb Rainier." *The Seattle Times*, 12 August 1990.

Whitney, Marci. "Notable Women: First Woman to Climb Rainier." *The Tacoma News Tribune*, 15 February 1976.

Special Thanks to:

Longmire Library employees, especially Kathleen Jobson, National Park Service, Mount Rainier National Park.
Alex Van Steen, Veteran Rainier Summit Guide with Rainier Mountaineering, Inc., and Alex Van Steen Expeditions, LLC.

MOTHER JOSEPH

Acceptance of The Statue of Mother Joseph. Presented by the state of Washington, I May 1980. Washington, D.C.: U.S. Government Printing Office, 1980.

Archives Of The Sister Of Providence-Sacred Heart Province:

Letters from Mother Joseph to:

Mother Caron	November 16, 1856,
Mother Caron	December 4, 1856,
Mother Caron	December 21, 1856,
Bishop Bourget	December 29, 1856,
Father Truteau	April 19, 1857,
Mother Caron	May, 1857,
Mother Caron	June, 1857,
Bishop Larocque	August 15, 1857,
Bishop Bourget	December 27, 1857,
Bishop Bourget	December 18, 1858,
Bishop Bourget	January 30, 1861,
Bishop Larocque	March 3, 1862,
Father Brouillet, V.G.	January 2, 1863,

Annals of Sisters of Providence:

1861—p. 142, 145, 147

Collections in The Mines Of Idaho and Montana
1866—p. 207, 210, 222

Begging Tours
1867—p. 224
1873—p. 303

House Of Providence Building
1873—p. 327
1874—p. 329, 370-371
1877—p. 230, 235, 274

Diary written on The Sea Voyage, November 2, 1856—translated by Sister Martin, and Sister Mary Barbara.

Annals of Providence Academy:

Mother Joseph—December 26, 1843-Entrance, p. 372

Chronicles Of Saint Joseph Hospital, Vancouver, Washington, Vol. 8, 1858-1952. Translated by Sister Dorothy Lentz, S.P. 1978.

Letter Of Chief Selstice Of The Coeur d' Alenes to Sister Catherine, 1870.

The Institute Of Providence Vol. I—1800-1844

Lucia, Ellis. *Seattle's Sisters of Providence*. Seattle: Providence Medical Center, Sisters of Providence, 1978.

McCrosson, Sister Mary. *The Bell and the River*. Seattle: Sisters of Charity of Providence, 1957 and 1986.

Tucker, Joan Pinkerton—"Beggar/Builder," video tape produced by KWSU Productions, Written and Narrated by Joan Pinkerton Tucker, 1993.

Special Thanks to:

Sisters Of Providence Archives, Sacred Heart Province, Seattle, Washington.
Loretta Zwolak Greene, Archivist.
Sister Rita Bergamini, S.P., Archivist Assistant.

BERTHA KNIGHT LANDES

Arnold, William. "Exhibit on Seattle's First Woman Mayor." *Seattle Post-Intelligencer*, 5 July 1974.

"Bertha Knight Landes." Obituary. *The Seattle Times*, 30 November 1943.

Cunningham, Ross. "Seattle's First-and-Only Woman Mayor." *The Seattle Times*, 20 December 1972.

Pieroth, Doris H. "Bertha Knight Landes: The Woman Who Was Mayor." In *Women In Pacific Northwest History*, edited by Karen Blair. Seattle: University of Washington Press, 1988. First published in *Pacific Northwest Quarterly*, 75 (July 1984).

Stockley, Tom. "Seattle's Woman Mayor." *The Seattle Times*, 14 July 1974.

Stripling, Sherry. "Folk Heroines: They Helped Build Pacific Northwest." *The Seattle Times*, 6 March 1985.

Suffia, David. "When Doc Brown's Cigar Thwarted a Reform Move." Seattle Historical Vignettes. *The Seattle Times*, 7 January 1974.

"Ten Take Their Places in State's History." *The Seattle Times*, 11 November 1985.

Watson, Emmett. "Big Bertha." *The Seattle Times*, 21 February 1984.

DR. MARY ARCHER LATHAM

By the Falls: Women of Determination. American Association Of University Women, Spokane Branch, 1989.

"Dr. Latham Flees in Open Buggy." *Seattle Post-Intelligencer*, 27 July 1905.

"Dr. Latham in Hands of Jury." *The Spokesman-Review*, 18 June 1905.

"Dr. Latham Is in Serious Plight." *The Spokesman-Review*, 14 June 1905.

"Dr. Latham Is Starving." *The Spokesman-Review*, 2 July 1905.

"Dr. Mary A. Latham." Annual Illustrated Supplement To *The Spokane Spokesman*, 1 Jaunuary 1892.

"Dr. Mary Latham Creates a Scene." *The Spokesman-Review*, 30 June 1905.

"Dr. Mary A. Latham Dead." *Spokane Chronicle*, 20 January 1917.

"Dr. Mary A. Latham Is Found Guilty." *The Spokesman-Review*, 19 June 1905.

Edwards, Rev. Jonathan. *History Of Spokane County*. W.H. Lever, Publishers, 1900.

"Former Friend Hurts Dr. Latham." *The Spokesman-Review*, 13 June 1905.

Inmate Register and File on Dr. Mary Latham, State Penitentiary at Walla Walla, Washington, Washington State Archives, 9 January 1906.

"James Latham." Obituary. *The Spokesman-Review*, 21 April 1903.

Latham v. Latham. Spokane County Superior Court file, Cause No. 9886, 1895.

"Mary A. Latham Faces a Jury." *The Spokesman-Review*, 10 June 1905.

"Messner Woos As Shop Burns, Bad Day For Defense." *The Spokesman-Review*, 17 June 1905.

"Own Witness Hurts Dr. Latham." *The Spokesman-Review*, 16 June 1905.

"Pioneer Woman Physician Succumbs to Pneumonia." *The Spokesman-Review*, 21 January 1917.

State Of Washington vs. Mary A. Latham. Spokane County Superior Court file, Cause No. 2438, filed 17 May 1905.

Special Thanks to:

Clerks of the Spokane County Superior Court, Spokane, Washington.
Nancy Gale Compau, Librarian, Northwest Room Spokane Public Library.
Karen De Seve, Curator of Special Collections, Cheney Cowles Museum (Eastern Washington State Historical Society Museum).
David Hastings, Chief of Archival Services, Washington State Archives.

LIZZIE ORDWAY

Binns, Archie. *Northwest Gateway: The Story of the Port Of Seattle*. Garden City, NY: Doubleday, Doran & Company, Inc., 1941.

Evans, Walter. "The Mercer Girls." Dateline: Northwest. *Seattle Post-Intelligencer*, 7 September 1975.

"First U. of W. President's Installation." *The Seattle Times*, 21 February 1928.

Fish, Byron. "Retired Teachers Will Pay Tribute at Mercer Girl's Grave." *The Seattle Times*, 12 May 1954.

Grant, Frederic J. *History of Seattle, Washington*. New York: American Publishing & Engraving Company, 1891.

Kitsap County History. Silverdale, WA: Kitsap County Historical Society Book Committee, 1977.

"Mercer's Speech." *Puget Sound Weekly*, 28 May 1866.

Perry, Fredi. *Port Madison Washington Territory 1854-1889*. Bremerton, WA: Perry Publishing, 1989.

BIBLIOGRAPHY

Perry Fredi, ed. *Kitsap County: The Year Of The Child 1979.* Silverdale, Wash.: Kitsap County Historical Society, 1979.

"Pioneer Career Woman." *The Seattle Times,* 6 July 1947.

Warren, James. "Miss Lizzie Tamed the West's Children." *Seattle Post-Intelligencer,* 6 April 1980.

Special Thanks to:

Claire Raaum, State Association of the Daughters of the Pioneers of Washington.

PANG YEE CHING

Angel Island: Ellis Island Of the West. Angel Island Immigration Station Foundation, http://www.a-better.com/angel.island.htm

"Chinese Workers Played Roles." *The Spokesman-Review,* 14 July 1940.

Cowles, Cheney. "Chinese Community Concepts Changing." *Spokane Daily Chronicle,* 24 June 1972.

Lowe, Felicia, Daniel Quan, and Ann Williams. *Gateway to Gold Mountain: A Journey Remembered.* Pamphlet. San Francisco: San Francisco Public Library, July 1-November 30, 1996.

Golden Legacy, A Chinese Historical and Cultural Project, Golden Legacy Web Page, http://www.kqed.org/from KQED/Cell/golden/ glmenu.html, KQED Instructional Television, San Francisco, CA.

The Annals of the Chinese Historical Society of the Pacific Northwest, Publications Editor 1983-1985 Douglas W. Lee, 1984

Lill, Lucille Lee, and Mark, Joyce Lee—Interviews,1997 and Written records, 1996.

"Yee C. Lee." Obituary. *The Spokesman-Review,* 7 January 1993.

Powers, Dorothy. "Lee Yuen Believes in His Herbs, 7 Children, 5 Grand children." *The Spokesman-Review,* 1951.

"Spokane Chinese Leader Dies at 82." *The Spokesman-Review,* 10 October 1972.

"Trio of Chinese Laid Northern Pacific Ties." *The Spokesman-Review*, 12 August 1945.

White, Aubrey L. "Chinese Burials of Early Day Recalled by Dwight." *The Spokesman-Review*, 6 December 1943.

Special Thanks to:

Lucille Lee Lill and Joyce Lee Mark, Mrs. Lee's daughters.
Nancy Gale Compau, Northwest Room of the Spokane Public Library.

KATHLEEN ROCKWELL

Browning, Robert. "Klondike Kate of Gold Rush Fame Dies at 77." *Seattle Post-Intelligencer*, 22 February 1957.

Kilroy, George. "Alaskans of Other Days." *The Alaska Weekly*, 14 August 1931.

"Klondike Kate Finds North Only Memory." *Seattle Post-Intelligencer*, 4 August 1933.

"Klondike Kate Flies North to Seek Word of Husband." *The Seattle Times*, 21 October 1946.

"Klondike Kate, Here for Fete, Rolls Cigarette, Reminisces." *The Seattle Times*, 29 November 1937.

"Klondike Kate Home as Bride." *Seattle Post-Intelligencer*, 22 July 1933.

"Klondike Kate, 65 and Happy, Returning to Wilds She Loves." *The Seattle Times*, 16 August 1944.

"Klondike Kate Succumbs at Home in Oregon." *The Seattle Times*, 21 February 1957.

Mann, May. "I Was Queen of the Klondike." *The Alaska Sportsman*, August (1944): 10–11, 28–32.

Rockwell, Kathleen—Obituary. *The Alaska Sportsman*, May (1957): 28–29.

"Rush Leaves Klondike Kate Cold." *Oregonian*, 26 October 1948.

Schillios, Rolv. "Dance Hall Girl." *The Alaska Sportsman*, March (1956): 8–11, 30–33.

———. "Dreams and Reality." *The Alaska Sportsman*, April (1956): 16–19, 38–41.

Rochester, Junius. "Seattle's Gift to Vaudeville, Alexander Pantages." *The Weekly*, 29 February–March (1984): 34–35.

Stanton, Patty. "Kate's Vivid Career in Klondike Recalled." *The Seattle Times*, 15 July 1973.

Stockley, Tom. "Klondike Kate: 'Queen of the Goldrush." *The Seattle Times*, 25 June 1972.

"Uses Her Money Then Jilts the Girl." *The Seattle Times*, 2 May 1905

Welch, Doug. "1937 Girls Shock Klondike Kate." *Seattle Post-Intelligencer*, 19 November 1937.

"Whitehorse—Letters, Photographys." *Alaska Magazine*, December 1973, A3.

OLIVE SPORE RYTHER

Andrews, Mildred Tanner. *Seattle Women: A Legacy of Community Development.* Seattle: The Seattle YWCA, 1984.

Chase, Cora G. *Unto The Least.* Seattle: Shorey Books, 1972.

Davis, Nancy Parker. "Memory of Great Woman Lives in Ryther Center." *The Seattle Times*, 16 June 1946.

Dennis, Juanita. "Growing Up with Mother Ryther." *The Seattle Times*, 29 October 1972.

Jacobsen, Berne. "Mrs. Ryther, Mother to All Children, Dies." *Seattle Post-Intelligencer*, 3 October 1934.

"Mother Ryther, Children Home Leader, Dead." *The Seattle Times*, 2 October 1934.

Ryther Child Center. Brochures. Seattle: Ryther Child Center, 1995–1997.

Suffia, David. "Mother Ryther: 3,000 Children Kept Her Young." *The Seattle Times*, 22 December 1974.

Thomas, Leah. "Let Not Your Heart Be Troubled, Children." *The Seattle Times*, 5 October 1934.

Special Thanks to:

Mary Anne Howard, Director of Community Relations, Ryther Child Center.

REAH MARY WHITEHEAD

Bechdolt, Jack. "Judge Reah Whitehead Sums Up Her Position." *Seattle Post-Intelligencer*, 10 October 1915.

"First Woman Judge Here, Reah Whitehead, Dies." *The Seattle Times*, 15 October 1972.

"Justice Reah M. Whitehead Resigns." *The Seattle Times*, 10 November 1941.

"Miss Reah Whitehead Takes Position on Bench." *Seattle Post-Intelligencer*, 12 January 1915.

"Miss Whitehead Honored by U.S. Women." *The Seattle Times*, 8 March 1926.

Neighbors, Dorothy. "Successful Seattle Women." *The Seattle Times*, 23 February 1941.

Suffia, David. "Reah Whitehead, Pioneer Woman Justice of Peace." *The Seattle Times*, 3 January 1975.

Starbuck, Dr. Susan. "Yesterday's Women Judges: Role Models for Today." *Judiciary*, (winter/spring 1985): 7.

Dumett, Ray. "The Washington Alumnus--Personality Sketch." University of Washington Alumni Association, January 1925.

"Woman to be Named as Assistant Prosecutor." *Seattle Post-Intelligencer*, 28 November 1908.

"Women Lawyers Meet." *The Seattle Times*, 10 August 1947.

Whitehead, Reah. "Women Succeed in Law—Find It Good Background." *The Seattle Times*, 7 February 1926.

Special Thanks to:

Robert Henderson, Public Information Officer, Office of the Administrator for the Courts.

BIBLIOGRAPHY

NARCISSA PRENTISS WHITMAN

Barto, Harold E. and Catherine Bullard. *History of the State of Washington.* Boston: D.C. Heath and Company, 1947.

Beaver, Lowell J. *Historic Memories from Monuments and Plaques of Western Washington.* Historic Memories, 1960.

Bennett, Robert A. *We'll All Go Home in the Spring.* Walla Walla, Wash.: Pioneer Press Books, 1984.

Dodd, Lawrence. *Narcissa Whitman on the Oregon Trail.* Fairfield, Wash: Ye Galleon Press, 1986.

Nixon, Oliver W. *How Marcus Whitman Saved Oregon.* Chicago: Star Publishing Company, 1895.

Sager, Catherine, Elizabeth Sager, and Matilda Sager. *The Whitman Massacre of 1847.* Fairfield, Wash.: Ye Galleon Press, 1986.

Whitman, Narcissa. *The Letters of Narcissa Whitman 1836-1847.* Fairfield, Wash.: Ye Galleon Press, 1986

———. *My Journal.* Fairfield, Wash.: Ye Galleon Press, 1982.

Special Thanks to:

Glen Adams and Ye Galleon Press.

INDEX

INDEX

INDEX

ABOUT THE AUTHOR

Northwest native, L. E. Bragg, was born in the shadow of Mount Rainier and raised in the Greater Seattle Area. A graduate of the University of Washington, Ms. Bragg spent six years living and teaching school on the Colville Indian Reservation in eastern Washington. She and her family reside on the eastern shore of Lake Washington.

L. E. Bragg's books celebrate the history, scenery, and cultural diversity of the Pacific Northwest. Her first two books, *A River Lost* and *Seattle, City By The Sound*, are picture books written at a level for young readers, as well as for adults to enjoy reading aloud. *More Than Petticoats: Remarkable Washington Women* is a chapter book for young adult to adult readers.